PA26

CONTENTS

D-DAY
THE NORMANDY LANDINGS AND THE LIBERATION OF EUROPE

Anthony Kemp

THAMES AND HUDSON

Even during the dark days of the summer of 1940, when defeat seemed imminent, the British Prime Minister, Winston Churchill, realized the only way to defeat the Germans would be to bring their forces to battle in France. To do that, three things were necessary. First, the threat of a German invasion of Britain had to be removed; second, a new British army had to be trained and equipped; third and most important of all, American manpower and industrial might would have to be harnessed.

CHAPTER 1

THE ORIGINS OF 'OPERATION OVERLORD'

The British Prime Minister, Winston Churchill (opposite). Hitler's so-called Atlantic Wall (right).

The participation of over 250,000 men in the Normandy landings on 6 June 1944 was the greatest amphibious operation ever carried out. To many of the British and French troops who had had to be evacuated from Dunkirk in northern France only four years earlier – when the Germans seemed invincible – the sheer scale of D-Day would have been almost inconceivable.

Setting up Combined Operations

In 1940 there were no specialized ships available 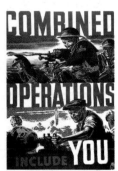 for landing troops and the British forces had no experience of amphibious operations. Churchill, however, was desperate to get to grips with the enemy, if only in a limited way, and to that end he established a new organization known as Combined Operations whose brief was to coordinate raids on the continent and test methods of invasion. At about the same time he called for the setting up of specially trained forces for amphibious assault, soon to be known as Commandos. In the spring of 1941 an ambitious raid, involving the landing of 1000 British Commandos, was carried out on the Lofoten Islands, which belonged to Norway.

The successful practice raids of the Commandos may have boosted morale at a time when Britain felt alone in its opposition to the might of the Nazi war machine, but they had little effect on the outcome. The tide began to turn, however, when Hitler, after overrunning Greece and Yugoslavia, ill-advisedly invaded Russia on 22 June 1941. He was now fighting on two fronts at once. The German armies swept forward to the gates of Moscow, but there they were brought to a standstill by the onset of the

brutal Russian winter. Hitler's fate was finally sealed later in the year. On 7 December 1941 his Japanese allies mounted a surprise attack on the US naval station in Pearl Harbor, Hawaii. Hitler misguidedly declared war on the United States four days later and America was committed to the Allied side.

Allied disagreement

At a conference in Washington, D.C., in January 1942, the Allies met to coordinate policy concerning the defeat of Germany. The responsibility for commanding the Allied war effort was given to a newly formed body, the Combined Chiefs of Staff. Within it strong differences of opinion surfaced. Churchill and his chiefs of staff favoured attacking

In September 1942 the German Sixth Army reached the city of Stalingrad. The Russian forces resisted and two months later mounted a strong counter-attack (left). The Germans were encircled. On 31 January 1943 Field-Marshal Friedrich von Paulus surrendered with 90,000 of his men. This was the turning-point of the war in the east.

The first large raid carried out by British Commandos was against the Norwegian-owned Lofoten Islands in March 1941 (below). Fish oil factories and 9000 tons of enemy shipping were destroyed by the 1000 men. As a result of that and similar raids in the area, on D-Day the Germans had 300,000 troops stationed in Norway rather than in France.

Germany through the Mediterranean. The Americans however, fearful of a total Russian collapse, argued for an all-out assault across the Channel in the hope of drawing maximum German forces away from the Red Army. The conference ended without any detailed agreement, but the Americans agreed to an exploratory landing in the Calais area during the summer of 1942 – 'Operation Sledgehammer' – and a large-scale invasion of France in

Captain Lord Louis Mountbatten (below) was put in command of Combined Operations in October 1941. He planned the invasion of Europe, then set for 1943, and also the raid on Dieppe.

LE REVEIL DU NORD

UNE ACTION DESESPÉRÉE SUR L'ORDRE DE MOSCOU

DANS LES ENVIRONS DE DIEPPE,

une grande tentative de débarquement anglo-américaine est brisée en 10 heures

1943 – 'Operation Roundup'. The British and Americans agreed about the need to help the Russians by creating a second front. Where they disagreed was whether this front should take the form of an all-out attack or a diversionary manoeuvre.
Given the lack of landing craft, and the fact that German submarines, the U-boats, were still masters of the Atlantic, such plans were somewhat academic. Without adequate shipping the massive movement of men and military equipment from America could not be accomplished.
Churchill was keen, however, to get American troops into action immediately and he proposed that in 1942 the Allies should instead concentrate on occupying the French colonies in North Africa – in 'Operation Torch'.

The failure of the Dieppe raid was a terrible blow to Allied morale, for it emphasized the fact that the Germans still seemed unbeatable. The beaches were littered with bodies and wrecked landing craft (top right). Although the Commando attacks on the flanks were successful, the assault on the town was a disaster and the Canadians lost 3379 men – either killed or taken prisoner. However, some valuable lessons were drawn and the Allies completely rethought their invasion plans for France.

The lessons of the Dieppe raid

An important event that greatly influenced the planning of subsequent landings in Normandy was the gallant but suicidal raid conducted by Canadian forces on the small French port of Dieppe in August 1942. The aim of the raid was to put a sizeable force ashore and to hold the port for a short period before re-embarking, in order to test the feasibility of a larger-scale invasion into France. It was also hoped that the Dieppe raid would tempt the Luftwaffe, the German air force, into the skies and force a battle, and might persuade the Germans to divert troops and aircraft from Russia.

The raid involved a frontal landing of a Canadian infantry division whose task it was to attack the town, and Commando forces, who landed on each flank to neutralize the gun batteries on the cliffs. As the Royal Navy was unwilling to risk heavy warships in the narrow waters of the Channel, there was no preliminary softening up of the defences. When the

The Dieppe raid was the first time that an attempt was made to land tanks to support an infantry assault during the war. The type used was the heavy British-designed Churchill Mark III (below). Only a few managed to move off the beach. Those that reached the town were stopped by concrete road blocks and disabled by enemy anti-tank guns.

Canadians disembarked, therefore, they were pinned down by the German artillery on the exposed beach and only a few of them managed to climb over the concrete sea-wall into the town. Most of the tanks proved incapable of surmounting this obstacle and remained behind on the beach with their tracks broken. Despite acts of individual gallantry, half the Canadian force who landed were killed, wounded or captured. The Germans were given plenty of good material for their propaganda machine, as they were able to claim that their forces had defeated a major invasion attempt.

The operation was a virtual disaster for the Allies, but did highlight for them the deficiencies in their plans for a cross-Channel assault. Several of the smaller types of landing craft used were made out of plywood. They were shot to pieces during the run-in, and hit the beaches with their crews dead or wounded. Communications between the headquarters ship and the units on shore were inept; the force commander had little idea of what was happening. It also became clear to the planners that tanks should not be landed unless specialized equipment was available to take them off the beaches. After the war Mountbatten commented that, for every soldier who died at Dieppe, ten were saved on D-Day.

More important, the Allied planners realized that a huge force would be needed at the point of attack, even if the invasion were to be launched over open beaches. It was also clear that to be able to unload sufficient men and supplies, it would be necessary to design artificial ports that could be towed over the Channel and assembled in the water off the beaches.

Dwight D. Eisenhower, or Ike, as he was known, was born into a poor family from Texas. A graduate from West Point in 1915, he had spent most of his army career before the Second World War in staff appointments. In 1942 he was sent to command Amercian forces in Britain and was named as the Allied commander of the landings in North Africa – 'Operation Torch' – (below). As the supreme commander of 'Operation Overlord', this calm, unassuming man, who commanded fierce loyalty, succeeded in holding the Allied armies together with his charm and diplomacy.

'Operation Torch'

Dieppe successfully killed further discussion of 'Sledgehammer' for 1942 and Churchill's enthusiasm for 'Operation Torch' grew as the planners concentrated their efforts on the landings in North Africa for November 1942. Meanwhile, General Sir Bernard Montgomery and the British Eighth Army won an outstanding victory far to the east on the Egyptian frontier at El Alamein in October 1942. There the German Field-Marshal Erwin Rommel and his Italian allies were decisively defeated. Then began a long and hectic campaign that ended when Montgomery's men linked up with 'Torch' forces in Tunisia to force the final surrender of the remaining German troops in North Africa in May 1943.

The supreme commander selected by the Allies for the African campaign was a relatively unknown American brigadier-general, Dwight D. Eisenhower, a capable staff officer whose highest troop command to date had been that of a battalion. Hastily promoted to general, Eisenhower

Field-Marshal Erwin Rommel (below), a German hero of the First World War, was put in command of the 7th Panzer Division during the campaign in France in 1940. A skilled tank commander, he was sent to lead the Afrika Korps in North Africa in 1941. Defeated at El Alamein in October 1942, he was ordered to return to Germany by Hitler. At the end of 1943 he was appointed to command Army Group B, with responsibility for the defence of Normandy against the Allied invasion.

formed an Allied staff, which included an American deputy (General Mark Clark) and three British deputies for air (Air-Chief Marshal Sir Arthur Tedder), sea (Admiral Sir Bertram Ramsay) and ground (Field-Marshal Sir Harold Alexander) operations. The logistical problem was immense in that the troops and supplies all had to be brought to the area by sea, subject to constant threat from German submarines and land-based bombers. Also the American forces had been hastily assembled and some units were only partially trained.

The Allies had pinned their hopes on General Henri Giraud taking power in Africa and therefore had had him smuggled out of France in November 1943, just before the 'Torch' landings. However, he proved to be unacceptable to the local regime, which remained loyal to Vichy France – the government of France established in the central city of Vichy after an armistice was declared with Germany – and Eisenhower was forced to deal with the collaborator, Admiral Darlan, who happened to be in Algiers at the time. The deal struck with Darlan, who was assassinated a few weeks later, provoked the anger of General Charles de Gaulle, leader of the Free French, who was equally unacceptable to the French authorities in the region. At the insistence of the Allies, de Gaulle and Giraud were forced to shake hands at Casablanca in January 1943, but the rivalries between the different French factions were to continue to cloud the political horizon.

There were three actual landings – at Algiers, Oran and Casablanca – which met only token resistance from the Vichy French authorities in Algeria and Morocco. In military terms 'Operation Torch' was a success. The Allies now had a stable springboard for launching operations against German-held areas in the Mediterranean.

At the conference held at Casablanca in January 1943 the two main Western leaders, Winston Churchill and President Franklin D. Roosevelt, tried to settle future strategy. The Allies had to contend with rivalries between the French factions over who was to lead the French Resistance. Watched by the two leaders, General Charles de Gaulle, head of the Free French, and General Henri Giraud, high commissioner of French North and West Africa, make a temporary reconciliation.

COSSAC: the architects of D-Day

In January 1943, the British Prime Minister, Winston Churchill, the American President, Franklin D. Roosevelt, and the Combined Chiefs of Staff met at Casablanca in Morocco. Although Eisenhower was given the authority to plan an invasion of Sicily, it was decided that preparations for 'Operation Roundup' should continue. An Anglo-American headquarters, headed by Lieutenant-General Sir Frederick Morgan, was set up in London to plan for the full-scale invasion of France – which was now postponed to early 1944 – to be known as 'Operation Overlord'. His new title was chief of staff to the supreme Allied commander (who had not yet been appointed) and his team therefore became known under the acronym COSSAC.

Morgan was able to call upon the experiences of those who had been responsible for the 'Torch' landings and the team that had been preparing for 'Sledgehammer', but otherwise had to start from scratch. From the outset, the planners were faced by a serious lack of naval equipment, as the enemy submarines were still sinking more tonnage than could be replaced by the shipyards in the early months of 1943. Gradually the battle of the Atlantic was won, however, and in American shipyards the techniques of mass-production pioneered by the motor industry were applied to the construction of standardized cargo vessels, known as Liberty ships.

In building the 'Liberty' ships that would ferry men and supplies across the Atlantic, the Americans put their genius for improvisation to good use. Special shipyards working day and night mass-produced in record time cargo vessels known as Liberty ships. Traditional methods of construction were abandoned in favour of welding the ships together in sections, using unskilled labour.

Where to land?

A series of factors had to be taken into consideration as the Allied planners determined where the actual invasion would take place. The shortest route would be the logical choice, as it would mean less time at sea, faster resupply and easier air support from airfields in England. The obvious choice was the Pas-de-Calais area. The Germans, realizing this, had concentrated their heaviest defences there. Knowing this, and believing the Pas-de-Calais to be virtually impregnable, the Allies instead selected the beaches of Normandy, some 240 kilometres to the southwest. Another drawback of the Pas-de-Calais region was that there were no large harbours on a par with those at Le Havre or Cherbourg (on the Cotentin Peninsula).

The COSSAC team finally opted for four specific beaches – code-named Omaha, Gold, Juno and Sword – on the northern coast of the Cotentin Peninsula in Normandy between the Orne and Vire rivers. Because of the limited resources originally allocated to 'Overlord', Morgan's planners produced a scheme to drop two airborne and to land three infantry divisions there, with two in reserve. The plan was agreed at a conference held at Quebec in August 1943, although Anglo-American differences about strategy continued to sour the atmosphere. The Americans wanted to divert landing craft to the Pacific, while Churchill urged a landing in Italy, where the Mussolini regime had just collapsed.

For the Allies, the Pas-de-Calais (right) was the obvious place to land, as it was close to both the industrial centres of Germany and airfields in England.

Below: German soldiers at the Atlantic Wall.

LONDON

Dover

Southampton Portsmouth Newhaven
Shoreham   Hastings   Calais
                                Boulogne
Portland-   Le Touquet
Weymouth   *Isle of Wight*

△ Radar   Dieppe   *GERMAN*
                        Fécamp   *FIFTEENTH*
● German battery   *ARMY*
                        Le Havre
★ Panzer Division
                Arromanches   Rouen
▨ Mines   Cherbourg
                Carentan   Ouistreham
            Saint-Lô Bayeux   Caen
                                        Évreux   PARIS
                        Falaise
            Avranches
Saint-Malo   *GERMAN SEVENTH ARMY*
        Mortain

The opposition

After the German armies overran France in the summer of 1940, they remained in occupation of the entire coast. The territory allocated to the Vichy regime was confined to the interior. Originally the French coast was seen as a springboard for a German invasion of Britain, but with the abandonment of that aim and the attack on Russia, it became clear that only small numbers of troops could be left in the west. Hitler decided therefore to fortify the coastline to deter British landings, and the defeat suffered by the Canadians at Dieppe seemed to prove him right. When America entered the war, however, Hitler realized that it was only a matter of time before a serious invasion attempt took place.

Field-Marshal Karl Gerd von Rundstedt was the German supreme commander in the west entrusted with the defence of a frontier of some 5000 kilometres stretching from the North Sea to the Mediterranean. With no clear idea of where the Allies might decide to land, he was forced to give priority to certain sectors and virtually ignore others. Construction of coastal fortifications known as the Atlantic Wall began seriously in early 1942 mainly in the Pas-de-Calais and around the major ports. Along the coast to the south of

Field-Marshal Karl Gerd von Rundstedt, the supreme commander in the west, was given the task of defending the Atlantic Wall, of which he said: 'The strength of the defences was absurdly overrated. The "Atlantic Wall" was an illusion; conjured up by propaganda – to deceive the German people as well as the Allies.'
Quoted in Sir Basil Liddell Hart, *The Other Side of the Hill*, 1951

The Germans developed their own radar sets (top left) early in the war and installed them along the French coast.

Calais, several heavy gun batteries capable of firing across the Channel were placed under huge concrete bunkers.

From hundreds of bunkers built along the coastline gunners were able to fire directly on to the beaches. They were supported by infantry strongpoints connected by underground passages. Radar stations were sited to give early warning of the enemy, but in many cases communications with rear headquarters relied on telephone wires.

A German soldier keeps watch from a typical Atlantic Wall beach defence.

Engineering for 'Overlord'

One of the first priorities of the Allied planners was to develop artificial harbours that could be assembled in England and towed across the Channel. A team, formed of the most fertile brains in the construction industry, soon devised the so-called Mulberry harbours under conditions of extreme secrecy. Construction involved a huge labour force of thousands of men housed in camps all along the south coast of England.

A further problem for the planners was how to ensure an adequate supply of petrol to the mainland. The answer was provided by a project known as PLUTO, short for 'pipeline under the ocean'. Two versions were tested, one a flexible hollow cable and the other, consisting of sections of metal pipe welded together that could be coiled into a large drum. Pumping stations were built on the south coast of the Isle of Wight, and in August 1944, two pipelines were laid across the Channel to Cherbourg to supply the Allied armies with much-needed petrol in the break-out phase of the campaign.

The Allied planners realized that infantry could not survive on open beaches without armoured support, and that special tanks would have to be designed to deal with

One of the floating drums (above left) that carried the PLUTO pipeline. As they were towed they unrolled slowly and the pipe sank to the seabed. To protect the open beaches, a number of old vessels were sunk to form breakwaters, known as Gooseberries, inside which ships could anchor in calm water. The main protection of the artificial Mulberry harbours consisted of a line of concrete caissons known as Phoenixes (above right), each weighing 600 tons, which were towed across the Channel and flooded to form a solid barrier. Inside the port, ships could tie up beside pierheads (Spuds) with massive legs positioned on the seabed.

bunkers and minefields, to fill in anti-tank ditches and to position bridges. Churchill put Major-General Percy Hobart in charge of the development of a range of specialist armour, which was consolidated into the 79th Armoured Division in 1943. The vehicles that Hobart's organization designed made a vital contribution to the overall success of D-Day and became known affectionately as his menagerie or his funnies.

The Allied chiefs of staff: SHAEF

At the supreme headquarters of the Allied expeditionary force (SHAEF), the choice of the supreme commander depended on political horse-trading between the Americans and the British.

Major-General Percy Hobart, the creator of the special types of tank known as funnies, was Montgomery's brother-in-law. Dieppe had taught that engineers could not work on open beaches without protection from fire and in early 1943 he was given the job of developing methods of protecting them. The Crocodile was a Churchill tank fitted with a long-range flamethrower. It towed an armoured trailer full of napalm. The Crab was a Sherman tank, on the front of which was a rotating drum fitted with lengths of chain which could beat a path through a minefield.

Some examples of Hobart's funnies. Opposite top: the flame mortar, which could fire a large container full of napalm. Opposite bottom: the Crocodile, one of the weapons most feared by the German soldiers. A huge jet of flame could be directed into the firing slits of bunkers. Above: a Bobbin tank, which could unroll a strip of canvas over soft patches of sand. Left: a Bobbin tank in action.

However, it was finally agreed at the Quebec conference in August 1943 that he would have to be an American, in view of the preponderance of American forces and equipment that would be involved. The choice finally fell on General Eisenhower, who was appointed in early December 1943. As his deputy, the British Air-Chief Marshal Sir Arthur Tedder, the commander in chief of the Allied air forces in the Mediterranean, was chosen. The post of naval commander in chief was given to the British Admiral Sir Bertram Ramsay, who had planned the 'Torch' landings in Africa. For the tactical air forces, the Air-Marshal Trafford Leigh-Mallory, also British, was selected.

General Dwight D. Eisenhower (left) would have preferred General Sir Harold Alexander (right) as ground forces commander for 'Overlord' in place of Montgomery, but it was felt that Alexander was needed in Italy. As commander in chief in the Middle East, he was Montgomery's superior. Air-Chief Marshal Sir Arthur Tedder (centre) was in charge of the Allied air forces and Eisenhower's deputy for 'Overlord'. A flying ace from the First World War, Tedder was given the job of coordinating the air and ground forces. By isolating the Normandy battlefields, Tedder's air force played a major role in the liberation of France.

The selection of a suitable ground commander, however, gave rise to controversy. Eisenhower's first choice would have been General Sir Harold Alexander, but Churchill felt that he should remain in Italy. Instead, General Sir Bernard Montgomery was appointed. The commander of the British Eighth Army and the victor over Rommel at El Alamein, Montgomery was a small, wiry, headstrong man. He had been under Eisenhower's command during 'Operation Torch'. Although extremely arrogant, he was possessed of an iron will to defeat his enemies in battle. Questions regarding his character were later to lead to bitter contention.

SHAEF established itself in Britain to the west of London in early 1944 with all the responsibilities for the Allied build-up of men and supplies. The movement of American troops into Britain was in full swing, and the soldiers had to be housed, fed and trained.

Montgomery arrived in Britain in January and found himself the inheritor of the original COSSAC plan, which he regarded as essentially flawed. He saw that the front had to be widened and the number of divisions to be landed increased from three to five to permit an extension of the invasion to the west of the Vire River, and Cherbourg to be captured more rapidly. There was, however, a severe shortage of landing craft. The invasion date, set for 1 May 1944, had to be postponed to June to allow the shipyards time to turn out enough craft.

Deception and 'Operation Fortitude'

Having chosen the place of invasion, the Allies had to persuade the Germans that it would take place elsewhere. This subterfuge was code-named 'Operation Fortitude'. The aim was to mask the arms build-up on England's south coast and concentrate German minds on England's southeastern coast, opposite the Calais area. Enemy reconnaissance missions were manipulated by Allied air

Admiral Sir Bertram Ramsay (below) was made Allied naval commander in chief for 'Operation Overlord' in 1944. The architect of 'Operation Neptune', the naval phase of 'Overlord', Ramsay was responsible for putting a million men and their supplies ashore from 6 to 12 June 1944. He was killed in an air crash in January 1945.

For beach reconnaissance a British X-class mini submarine (left) was used. In addition to the crew of three, two frogmen and their equipment had to be carried. On the night of 17 January 1944, two swimmers landed at Vierville to investigate the sand. A German sentry walked right past them, treading on the hand of one of them. Three days before the actual invasion, two such submarines submerged off the British beaches. At dawn on 6 June they came to the surface and activated radio beacons to guide in the landing craft.

superiority and certain German aircraft were 'permitted' to fly over Kent, where they could photograph masses of 'tanks' and 'landing craft'. The fact that these were actually inflatable rubber dummies, or made of plywood and canvas, was not apparent from the air and enemy intelligence was easily taken in.

Another part of the deception plan was the creation of a false headquarters known as the 1st US Army Group, supposedly commanded by General George S. Patton, based around Dover in Kent, and complete with fake radio traffic. The Germans knew of the American general's reputation as a fighting commander, but were unaware of his true role – to take command of the US Third Army in Normandy during the break-out phase.

On D-Day itself convoys of small craft sailed up the Channel towards the Dieppe area equipped with radar devices to simulate the movement of a much larger convoy. These measures kept the Germans in ignorance of the true destination of 'Overlord' until the actual bombardment started – and, indeed, for some time after.

Apart from information from the French Resistance and the evidence of air photography, the Allies desperately needed information about the types of obstacles planted on the beaches by the Germans and the thickness of the sand. Fortunately, specialist teams, known as COPP or Combined Operations Pilotage Parties, were at hand. They were made up of two-man teams of frogmen who were able to land silently from canoes or miniature submarines. COPP made a number of clandestine visits to the Normandy beaches in early 1944, bringing back samples of the sand and details of the various obstacles. At the end of February such visits were stopped, as it was feared that if anything went wrong and men were captured, attention might be drawn to the area.

A full-size inflatable Sherman tank carried by its 'crew' was just one of the examples of the successful effort that was put into deceiving the enemy as to where the invasion would take place in 'Operation Fortitude'. Teams of soldiers equipped with such devices and an air compressor moved around at night to create an illusion of troop concentrations opposite the Calais area. Overnight, small harbours would be filled with 'landing craft' and fields with 'aeroplanes'. Expert set designers were recruited from the theatres to create camouflage effects and old merchant ships were made to look like tank landing craft.

No matter how good the military plan and the intelligence about the enemy, no army can fight a successful battle without first-class back-up and support. For every soldier firing a rifle in the front line, there may be as many as seven others behind him, keeping him supplied with everything that is necessary to maintain him in efficient fighting condition. The success of D-Day and the Normandy campaign relied heavily on the pre-invasion preparations.

CHAPTER 2

PREPARING FOR THE INVASION

While von Rundstedt (right) was enjoying the luxury of his château outside Paris, Allied troops all along the south coast of England practised embarking and disembarking from their landing craft (opposite).

By January 1944, the southern counties of England had been transformed into a vast military camp as the build-up of the necessary forces and material for the invasion began to reach its climax. The high-speed liners, the *Queen Mary* and the *Queen Elizabeth*, now painted a drab grey, had been pressed into service to transport thousands of Americans across the Atlantic. Nearly a million GIs were packed into the rural landscapes of Somerset, Devon and Dorset. On the whole it was a peaceful 'invasion', with little friction between the newcomers and the locals and numerous American expressions were absorbed into the everyday language.

The Canadians used huge areas of the Sussex Downs for their training. Hotels, guest-houses and schools were requisitioned for billeting, and the small harbours filled steadily with landing craft. To feed, house, supply and give medical attention to such huge numbers, a complex organization had to be established from almost nothing. The unsung heroes of D-Day were those men and women who organized the logistics – the endless lists of everything from tank engines to toilet paper, from French phrase books to complete mobile operating theatres – that made the invasion possible.

American officers having tea with the vicar in a Dorset village. This was one of many propaganda photos taken to show that the 'boys' were well-behaved.

One vital need was for areas where the
assault divisions could train realistically – using
live ammunition and landing on beaches similar to the
ones they would encounter in Normandy. A number of
coastal areas in the south of England were requisitioned
and their inhabitants, together with their household
possessions and livestock, had to move out. One such
area was Slapton Sands, near Dartmouth in Devon,
which was designated as an assault training zone, mainly
for use by American forces. Eight villages were
entirely evacuated by 20 September 1943
and afterwards all civilians were barred
from further entry.

In order to ensure that the right troops
embarked on the right landing craft from
the right port, a whole network of camps
was established near the coast in the
marshalling areas. Area A, to the north of Portsmouth,
for example, consisted of seventeen camps and seventy
kilometres of vehicle standing bays. These camps were
surrounded with miles of barbed wire, as, once inside,

American troops
marching through
an English village.
The GIs were given
a guidebook (inset) to
tell them about daily
life in England.

The American
Hershey chocolate
bar was a particular
favourite with children
in England.

the assault formations were to be briefed on their destination and all communication with the outside world was forbidden. In addition, huge supply depots had to be built, the narrow English roads widened, bridges strengthened to carry tanks, and hundreds of miles of extra railway sidings constructed. Pipelines were laid between the refineries and the south coast ports, where petrol would be loaded on to the tankers that would carry fuel across the Channel.

An additional complicated undertaking was the tabulation and organization of the loading plans for individual landing craft and ships, each of which had to deliver the right men and supplies to

One of the most important factors in ensuring the success of the landings was adequate training. Soldiers (opposite below) practise unarmed combat. Large areas of the countryside were reserved for manoeuvres and firing ranges. Conditions were made as realistic as possible, and the interaction between infantry and armoured units and air support had to be carefully coordinated.

There were also endless rehearsals in getting men and vehicles on and off landing craft in the right order. Even such simple matters as waterproofing rifles had to be learned. For certain units with specific missions – such as the capture of a German gun position – full-scale models of the target were built, complete with dummy bunkers and trenches.

the right place in the proper order. An assault formation was a finely balanced entity including infantry, armoured support vehicles, signallers, demolition engineers and medical teams. Once they were ashore, the second echelon had to arrive bringing more ammunition and

The supply services worked round the clock to stockpile vehicles and equipment.

vehicles, spare parts, petrol, rations, artillery and the cooks. Returning craft were to be filled with the wounded, prisoners of war and damaged vehicles.

Fine tuning

Y-Day was the date when everything had to be ready to go, awaiting only the supreme commander's decision. It had been set for 1 June, after which no further corrections could be made to the master plan. This date was revealed to a select audience consisting of the general staff, the senior planners and the actual assault commanders (down to divisional level), at the headquarters of the British 21st Army Group at St Paul's School in London on 15 May. Also present were King George VI and Winston Churchill. At the end of the proceedings General Eisenhower remarked, 'Hitler has missed his one and only chance of destroying with a single well-aimed bomb the entire high command of the Allied forces.'

Seated on hard school benches, the dignitaries faced a huge map spread out across one wall. Montgomery, although 'very quiet and deliberate' (in Eisenhower's words), totally dominated the proceedings. There

The faces of the Allied high command radiate unity of purpose here, yet their later quarrels cast a shadow over operations. From left to right: General Bradley, Admiral Ramsay, Air-Chief Marshal Tedder, General Eisenhower, General Montgomery, Air-Marshal Leigh-Mallory and General Bedell-Smith.

remained only three weeks before the invasion and there was little left for the senior commanders to do besides carry out a strenuous programme of visits to all the assault formations and those in the follow-up echelons.

While these visits were being carried out, SHAEF and the 21st Army Group were on the move to the countryside of Hampshire, just to the north of Portsmouth, where they set up camp in and around a large mansion, Southwick House, that had been requisitioned for use. It was from there that the decision to launch 'Operation Neptune', the naval phase of 'Overlord', would be made.

The work of the French Resistance

The French Resistance in France reflected the country's political divisions: there were Gaullist and Communist groups, and others with monarchist leanings. Responsibility for supplying the members of the Resistance lay largely in the hands of the British special operations executive (SOE), but just before D-Day, General Pierre-Joseph Koenig was recognized as head of the FFI (free French forces of the interior), in an effort to provide coordination between the various factions.

The French General Pierre-Joseph Koenig was appointed to command all of the various factions of the French Resistance who would help the Allies in France. The Allied planners harboured a fear that units of the Resistance with differing political opinions might end up fighting each other instead of the Germans. Support for the Resistance in France was organized by the special operations executive (SOE) in London, which was divided into several sections, including both the British and free French networks. On 1 July 1943 they were amalgamated into a single joint command under Koenig.

The Resistance forces in Normandy had been ordered by the Allies to keep a low profile, collect intelligence but not to provoke any violent reprisals. Their job during the invasion would be to slow down the movement of German armoured divisions into the battle area. To train and arm the Resistance, a large number of missions were dropped all over France, each consisting

Night after night, converted bomber aircraft flew by moonlight with their vital cargo of arms, ammunition and explosives. On the ground, tense groups of men and women – members of the Resistance – waited for the noise of the engines, before lighting their flares. When they spotted the parachutes, there was a mad rush to collect the containers before daylight.

SABOT

of two uniformed officers, British and/or American, accompanied by a radio operator. These teams were backed up by several larger groups of men from the Special Air Service Regiment, who were parachuted in with their jeeps to harry the enemy lines of communication in the interior of France. All over the country, small parties of patriotic French men and women began to sabotage the German war effort, suffering terrible losses in the process. Railways were destroyed, bridges demolished, communication lines cut and German officers assassinated. Locations of suitable bombing targets were radioed back to London.

Using plastic explosive placed under the rails – preferably on a curve, which was more difficult to repair – the members of the French Resistance destroyed strategic sections of railway lines.

The various pockets of the Resistance were instructed by means of personal messages broadcast by BBC radio in London. These usually took the form of two lines of a well-known poem. When the first line was broadcast, it meant that invasion was imminent and that the recipients should be prepared. When the second line was heard, the Resistance knew it was time to go into action against a list of targets previously agreed with London.

The German army suffers from an unwieldy command structure and conflicting personalities

The arrival of the German Field-Marshal Erwin Rommel on the scene in early January 1944 sparked off a flurry of

British-designed transmitter/receiver radios that fitted inside a normal suitcase were supplied to the Resistance networks together with trained operators, known as 'pianists'. Theirs was one of the most hazardous jobs, as the German intelligence teams could soon locate their positions.

activity along the occupied coastline, as the German troops were put to work constructing extra beach defences, flooding low-lying areas and planting sharpened stakes (known as Rommel's asparagus) in fields suitable for landing gliders. Enormous numbers of mines were laid, extra pillboxes built and pre-war fortifications were pillaged for such items as bullet-proof doors. Luckily for the Allies, the Germans were severely hampered by lack of troops and supplies to complete all the measures that the energetic field-marshal demanded.

Rommel was convinced that the only way to defeat an Allied landing was to do so before it could establish itself – in other words on the beaches.

Field-Marshal Rommel (below) during one of his frequent tours of inspection along the Normandy coast. Convinced of the need to defeat the invaders before they could reach the shore, he personally supervised much of the construction work of the Atlantic Wall.

A meeting of the German high command at the Hotel Prince de Galles in Paris on 8 May 1944. From left to right: General Geyr von Schweppenburg, commander of the Panzer Group West, General Blaskowitz of Army Group G, Field-Marshal Sperrle, the Luftwaffe commander in chief, Field-Marshal von Rundstedt, Field-Marshal Rommel and Admiral Kranke. Their topic of conversation was where the Allied landing would take place. Their intelligence reports told them it would be on 18 May.

A German bunker in Normandy camouflaged as a typical holiday villa. Local members of the French Resistance had provided the Allied planners with valuable information about the German defences.

To that end, he argued, the available armoured divisions should be stationed near the coast so as to be able to hit an invasion force as soon as possible. Aware as he was of the Allies' air superiority, he realized how difficult it would be to move reserves to the battle front once a successful landing had been carried out. However, his superior, the elderly Field-Marshal von Rundstedt, disagreed, believing that a strong central pool of armoured divisions should be kept well back from the front and then be used for a decisive counter-attack. He was supported by General Geyr von Schweppenburg, commander of the Panzer Group West.

The argument raged throughout the spring of 1944. Hitler, who was of course heavily involved in the decision-making, decided to form a reserve of four armoured divisions under his own control and to station them in the vicinity of Paris. Rommel was left with only three such divisions to cover the entire coast between the Scheldt and the Loire rivers. Although increasingly convinced of the possibility of an Allied landing in Normandy, he left two of his panzer divisions north of the Seine, and only one, the 21st Panzer, to the south of Caen. Its presence there proved decisive in the failure to capture that city on D-Day.

The defence of Normandy was the responsibility of the German Seventh Army, commanded by General Friedrich Dollmann. Many of the divisions manning the coastal defences were low-grade units, filled with elderly reservists and those who were generally unfit. Other units consisted of foreigner prisoners – Russians, Ukrainians, Cossacks, Tartars. Many of the German artillery pieces were captured weapons and thus lacked standard ammunition. Furthermore, lack of motor transport meant that the coastal divisions were condemned to fight a static battle. Almost all the senior German commanders were convinced, however, that the actual invasion would be to the north of the Seine, in the Pas-de-Calais area.

The landing ship tank (LST) was a large ocean-going vessel (above left), specially designed for landing tanks and trucks, while its smaller sister (above right), the landing craft tank (LCT) had a flat bottom and could run directly on to a beach to unload its tanks.

Practice runs –'Exercise Tiger' and 'Exercise Fabius'

As many of the assault units, especially the American ones, lacked combat experience, some realistic exercises – many of them with live ammunition – were carried out. They included shore bombardment by warships and manoeuvres using Allied aircraft. One such simulated assault was 'Exercise Tiger', conducted at the end of April, which consisted of a landing by the US 4th Infantry Division on Slapton Sands in Devon, followed by an advance inland to link up with the two American airborne divisions, the 101st and the 82nd. It was also designed as an exercise for Naval Force U, which would convey the men of the US VII Corps to Utah Beach in Normandy on D-Day. In all, 25,000 men and 2750 vehicles had to be moved, landed and then recovered after the three-day manoeuvre. Purely by chance, a group of German E boats (surface torpedo boats) from Cherbourg stumbled on one of the convoys approaching the area. They managed to sink two LSTs (specially designed landing vessels for tanks and

trucks) and severely damage three others before making off, causing nearly seven hundred American casualties. The immediate result was a fearful panic in case any personnel with knowledge of the invasion plan had been fished out of the water and taken prisoner.

As an exercise, 'Tiger' was shambolic. The commander of the engineer assault battalion was relieved on the spot, the medical services proved incapable of moving 'casualties' back to the beach and communications collapsed. As General Bradley reportedly remarked, 'It was more like a peacetime manoeuvre than a dress rehearsal of an assault against a continent'.

A few days later, 'Exercise Fabius' was mounted, with simulated landings at various points along the south coast of England. It proved to be generally satisfactory, and officers were able to iron out a lot of details.

This American LST (below) was badly damaged by torpedo fire from German E boats during 'Exercise Tiger'.

Overleaf: American soldiers (top) embark at Weymouth. German soldiers (bottom) on watch from the shelter of a bunker on the Atlantic Wall.

The 'sausage machine'

The 'sausage machine' was the nickname given to the marshalling system into which the men of the assault units were fed during the month of May, to emerge only when the orders to embark were given. All of the southern and much of the eastern coast of England had been declared off limits, travel in and out of the region – except for very urgent reasons – was banned. The marshalling camps, surrounded with barbed wire and guarded by armed sentries, penned in the men who were gradually briefed but not told their actual destination. The maps and models that were used all had the place-names blanked out and a false survey grid was printed on them. Plainclothes intelligence personnel moved around the area listening and watching for any signs of people talking too much. The invasion preparations could not be hidden from the local civilian population and the security authorities were desperately worried about German spies and possible information leaks.

In that final period there was much vital work to be done. All vehicles had to be waterproofed and weapons, especially new tanks, had to be test-fired and have their sights set. Supplies had to be stockpiled in the right place and the follow-up divisions had to be ready to move south as soon as the assault divisions had moved out. Each division on the battlefield required 600 tons of supplies per day in order to be able to fight. From distant harbours in Scotland, the slow moving old ships that would form the Gooseberry breakwaters had to start

The faces of these American GIs waiting to leave for France (below) show the strain imposed by months of training and the uncertainty about what awaited them in Normandy.

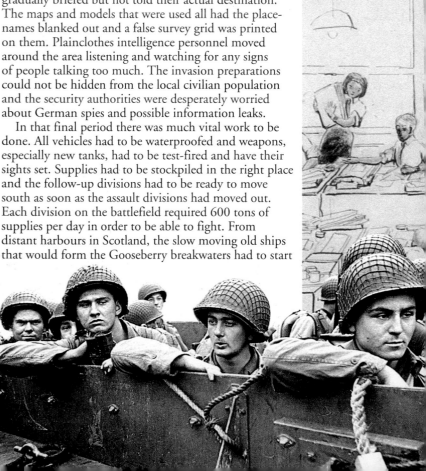

their last voyage. One alarm concerned the Phoenix caissons for the Mulberry, which had been sunk in shallow water near Portsmouth to hide them from German reconnaissance aircraft. When the time came to pump them out and raise them into position, ready for towing to France, it was discovered that the pumps were not strong enough. Specialists with heavy salvage equipment were rushed to the spot to avoid disaster.

At Norfolk House, the headquarters of 'Operation Neptune', Admiral Ramsay was assisted by the WRNS – the Women's Royal Naval Service – who took over the secretariat and communications.

Yet, like some vast mosaic, everything gradually fell into place – even adequate supplies of condoms were found for the ends of rifle barrels (to keep them free from sand and debris)! As a final precaution, two X-class miniature submarines headed for the coast of Normandy. There they were to lie submerged on the seabed until the invasion fleet approached, at which time they were to rise to the surface and activate radio beacons to mark the boundaries of the landings.

'Operation Neptune' and postponement

'Neptune' was the code-name for the naval plan, the first convoys of which had to start their move as early as 1 June. Admiral Ramsay, whose job it was to deliver the men, the tanks and the guns ashore, had a huge and extremely varied fleet under his command, from battleships to harbour tugs. It was predominantly a British force, since much of the US navy was occupied in the Pacific theatre. In addition to the bombarding force of 137 warships, there were over 4000 landing craft and ships of various types, 700 support craft and nearly 900 merchant vessels. In the lead on D-Day would be the minesweepers clearing channels for the five assault forces, one for each beach, under the command of a headquarters ship. The bombarding force of 6 battleships and 2 elderly British monitors (heavily armoured warships) would be backed up by 23 cruisers.

Ramsay was at the mercy of both weather and tides. As General Eisenhower said: 'We wanted to cross the Channel with our convoys at night so that darkness would conceal the strength and direction of our several attacks. We wanted a moon for our airborne assaults. We needed approximately forty minutes of daylight preceding the ground assault to complete our bombing and preparatory bombardment. We had to attack on a relatively low tide because of beach

obstacles which had to be removed while uncovered.'
In June, such conditions were available only between
the fifth and the seventh days of the month.

Embarkation of men and equipment began on 2 June,
but on 4 June a powerful storm – the worst in June in
twenty years, according to Eisenhower – was lashing the
south coast of England. At the regular briefings at
Southwick House, it was the chief meteorologist, Group-
Captain James Stagg of the Royal Air Force (RAF),
to whom great attention was paid, although the weight
of the actual decision rested solely on Eisenhower's
shoulders. Later in the day, Stagg was able to announce
there would be a brief improvement in the weather on
6 June. The final weather conference was held at 0400
hours on Monday. At 0415 hours Eisenhower, having
listened to the opinions of the other senior commanders,
spoke the now-famous words, 'OK. Let's go.'

Landing craft (top)
packed tightly in
Southampton docks.

Once he had made
the final decision
to launch 'Overlord',
Eisenhower had little to
do. On the evening of 5
June, he called for his
car and drove to the
airfield where the
men of the US 101st
Airborne Division
were preparing to leave
(opposite).'I stayed
with them until the
last of them were in
the air, somewhere
around midnight.'

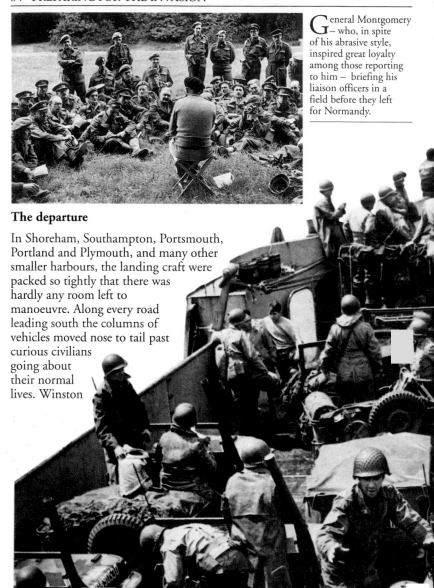

General Montgomery – who, in spite of his abrasive style, inspired great loyalty among those reporting to him – briefing his liaison officers in a field before they left for Normandy.

The departure

In Shoreham, Southampton, Portsmouth, Portland and Plymouth, and many other smaller harbours, the landing craft were packed so tightly that there was hardly any room left to manoeuvre. Along every road leading south the columns of vehicles moved nose to tail past curious civilians going about their normal lives. Winston

Churchill travelled on his special train to be near the action. He had intended to join one of the ships himself and turned a deaf ear to Eisenhower's pleas for a sense of responsibility. Only the king's wily arguments prevented Churchill from setting off for France on D-Day on board a destroyer.

The units of the assault fleet started to leave Southampton during the afternoon of 5 June, while those coming from further west had been at sea since the early morning. Every ship was heading to

⁶The 36-foot coffin-shaped steel boats took solid green sheets of water that fell on the helmeted heads of the troops packed shoulder to shoulder in the stiff, awkward, uncomfortable, lonely companionship of men going to a battle.⁹

Ernest Hemingway

a rendezvous point – which became known as Piccadilly Circus – just to the south of the Isle of Wight, from which all the various convoys would turn towards France. The inhabitants of the small port of Salcombe, which had been home to a flotilla of American landing craft, woke to find their harbour totally empty.

On the heaving vessels, commanding officers opened sealed envelopes as soon as they passed the outer defences of the harbours they were leaving. In them they found the final maps that named their true destinations. On the larger ships, church services were held, with attentive congregations, and will-forms were handed out. Many of those men who took part later wrote of a sense of unreality as they sailed into battle through the night.

In France Field-Marshal Rommel left in his staff car for a few days at home in southern Germany, as the various senior German commanders were all convinced that an invasion was unlikely, given the appalling weather conditions. In fact, many officers were absent from their command posts on the night of 5 June. After the main BBC news that night, a stream of personal messages was transmitted, and in the darkness, men and

British airborne troops embarking late in the evening of 5 June. British and American airborne troops left from airfields to the north-west of London. D-Day was the first time during the war that such large numbers of paratroopers had been dropped into action. The main type of aircraft used to transport paratroopers was the American DC3 Dakota. Hundreds of plywood gliders were towed across the Channel and then released at first light to glide down into the fields. Although many crashed, others landed safely and delivered their vital jeeps, men and light artillery.

women of the Resistance slipped out to play their small but crucial roles in 'Overlord'. A young woman who worked in the post office at Langrune-sur-Mer wrecked the telephone exchange before locking up and going home for the night. As she rode off on her bicycle she saw some German soldiers shooting at targets on the beach. 'You will be the targets tomorrow,' she thought.

As dusk fell, the airborne troops in England made their way to the waiting aircraft and gliders which were parked wingtip to wingtip at dozens of airfields. Eisenhower joked and chatted in the darkness with the men of 101st Airborne. The first British aircraft to leave was an Albemarle, carrying a group from the 22 Independent Parachute Company, whose task it was to find and mark the drop zones with flares and radio beacons.

A group of motor launches, equipped with radar devices that could simulate a much larger force, headed north up the Channel ostensibly for a landing between Dieppe and Boulogne. They were accompanied by bomber aircraft, who dropped strips of aluminum to confuse the German radar operators.

Two of the most important figures were destined to wait on the sidelines. Churchill (below left), who had planned to sail with the fleet on D-Day, was persuaded not to do so by King George VI. Eisenhower (below right), finally went to bed with a book, knowing there was nothing left for him to do.

The fleet of troop-carrying aircraft were the first away, heading for the drop zones on the Cotentin Peninsula. They flew in from the west over the Channel Islands, skirting the heavy concentration of flak based around Cherbourg. Even so there was enough anti-aircraft fire to unnerve many of the inexperienced pilots.

CHAPTER 3
D-DAY

As dawn broke on 6 June, German sentries looking out to sea from their bunkers saw that the horizon was black with ships. Alarm bells rang and sleepy men tumbled from their bunks. Soon they would be fighting for their lives as the landing craft disgorged men and tanks under a hail of fire. The Allies had achieved their aim of completely surprising the Germans.

The mission of American airborne operations was to cut off the Cotentin Peninsula. Major-General Matthew Ridgway's 82nd Airborne Division was due to drop in the area of the small town of Sainte-Mère-Eglise at 0100 hours on the morning of 6 June, but many of the 'sticks' of paratroopers were scattered all over the countryside, losing most of their heavy equipment in the process. Major-General Maxwell Taylor's 101st Airborne suffered equally badly. Their mission was to drop inland of the flooded area behind Utah Beach to secure the exit roads and the key bridges at Carentan, but many of the men were inadvertently dropped into the water and drowned with their heavy equipment.

Officers found it impossible to rally cohesive bodies of men and a series of small battles erupted all over the area as the enemy began to react. Disaster appeared imminent, but the sheer determination of the young American troops paid off as they regrouped and made their way towards the battle. The paradox was that the widely scattered drops caused confusion in the various German headquarters, as reports flooded in of paratroopers all over the peninsula. So many telephone lines had been cut by the French Resistance that the incoming reports failed to give a cohesive picture and the German corps commander, General Erich Marcks, was unable to take full control of the battle.

From midnight on, wave after wave of Dakotas flew over the Cotentin Peninsula and the paratroopers floated down into the dark countryside. In spite of the wide dispersal, enough men gathered to form a cohesive perimeter and repel the strong German counter-attacks. Major-General Ridgway, commanding the US 82nd Airborne Division, set up his first headquarters in an orchard. He later wrote: 'The Germans were all around us, of course, sometimes within 500 yards [460 metres] of my command post, but, in the fierce and confused fighting that was going on all about, they did not launch the strong attack that could have wiped out our eggshell perimeter defence.'

The insignia of the
American airborne
divisions – the
101st (below)
and the 82nd (bottom).

British airborne operations

As the Americans were landing, the British 6th Airborne
Division began to land to the east of Caen. One of the
leading formations was a detachment of six gliders under
the command of Major John Howard, whose hazardous
mission was to capture intact two bridges – one over the
Orne River and the other over the canal at Bénouville –
Pegasus Bridge. The gliders swooped down
silently in the dark, managing to land in the

right place. The paratroopers succeeded in overwhelming the German defenders, despite the opposition.

The rest of the division dropped to the east of the
Orne, and a firm defence perimeter was established.
Engineers demolished the fields of Rommel's asparagus,
enabling the gliders to land with vehicles, light artillery
and other weapons. At 0300 hours fleets of bombers
roared overhead to bomb the coastal defences with
thousands of tons of bombs. At 0500 hours the guns of
the warships signalled the arrival of the invasion fleet.

An aerial photograph of Merville battery (above) after it had been bombed. The wreckage of a glider (below) with Pegasus Bridge in the background. The operation was very successful – all six gliders landed close to their targets and the two vital bridges were taken with the loss of only one officer.

Although the advance units of 21st Panzer Division were in the area, their commander was absent in Paris. In the general confusion, no orders were issued for the division to attack until much later in the morning, by which time the chance to wipe out the fragile bridgehead that the British had established had been lost.

One of the main threats to the success of the whole D-Day operation came from the heavy coastal artillery batteries that the Germans had built with their guns sheltered in massive concrete bunkers. One of these batteries was at Merville, within the British airborne landing zone. The task of dealing with it was given to an airborne battalion commanded by Lieutenant-Colonel Terence Otway. Heavy Lancaster bombers, whose job was to deliver a preliminary softening up of the battery, missed and hit a field full of cows instead, and the raiding force was dropped haphazardly. Another integral part of the plan had been to land four gliders carrying an assault force on top of the battery, but the signal flares they needed to see their target were missing. As a result the gliders landed some distance away. Despite these difficulties, Otway, who was able to rally only 150 men, decided to proceed with the attack. Lacking the necessary explosives and heavy weapons, they stormed into the battery. Casualties were high, but the men managed to disable the guns on time.

While Allied aircraft dropped their bombs on the enemy defences, the naval bombardment force moved into position. Each ship had a specific target – a coastal battery or strongpoint – and above the fleet, aircraft spotted the accuracy of the firing. Huge shells rained down on the defenders, while the troops of the assault wave scrambled into their landing craft. The warships remained in position until the battle moved inland out of range.

The assault on the beaches

The presence of a huge assembly of ships off the coast of Normandy was noticed by German coastal radar, but no general alert was issued to the shore defences and no enemy aircraft appeared. Protected by the warships, the Allied assault formations lined up for the complicated approach on the beaches on the rough seas. The converted ships carrying the bulk of the infantry lowered the small LCAs (landing craft, assault) into which the heavily laden troops had to scramble. The various landing vessels lined up in a precise order. The entire assemblage was guarded by destroyers on each flank.

Getting the various components of a battalion together with its support weapons into the right place and in the right order was like a complicated ballet movement. As shells from the warships screamed overhead, it seemed to the seasick men aboard the landing craft that the whole beach was on fire.

In the lead went the LCS(M)s (landing craft support, medium) with forward artillery spotters to direct gunfire on to targets among the beach defences. Behind them came the amphibious, propeller-driven DD (duplex-drive) tanks. They were followed by a line of LCTs (landing craft, tank) loaded with specialist armour and then by the infantry in the LCAs. Accompanying the assault waves were special support landing craft armed with anti-aircraft guns to deter enemy planes, rocket-firing craft to saturate the defences and even 25 pounder (light) artillery – the so-called mosquito fleet or the small, fast-moving ships. Bringing up the rear were self-propelled guns that were able to fire during the approach.

For many of the men, tortured by seasickness, the prospect of finally reaching the shore to meet the enemy was preferable to remaining on a rough sea. The beaches on which they were to land were blanketed with smoke and flames, and remarkably little German fire was directed at the assembly points. At six o'clock on the morning of the sixth day of the sixth month of 1944 the liberation of France commenced.

Utah Beach

On the morning of D-Day Utah Beach was totally obscured by smoke from the bombardment. Some 30,000 men and 3500 vehicles were assembling offshore waiting for dawn. The weather was grim, with low scudding clouds and a strong offshore breeze.

General Hobart and his team developed the DD (duplex-drive) tank for that purpose, by fitting standard Sherman tanks with twin propellors. Rubberized canvas 'skirts' allowed the 33-ton tanks to float. Once on shore, the skirts were dropped and the tanks could operate normally. On D-Day many were launched too far out to sea and sank with their crews before they reached land.

Overleaf: the five beaches where the landings took place on 6 June 1944.

MERVILLE RANVILLE OUISTREHAM RIVA BELLA SAINT-AUBIN COURSEULLES CAEN

SWORD JUNO G

Daimler battery

anti-tank ditches

88 mm guns

anti-tank ditch

concrete wall

blockhouse

DD tanks

beach defences

LCA

hours

AHA

sur-Mer

Y DIVISION

0630 hours
OMAHA
Pointe du Hoc

US 2ND RANGER BATTALION

0630
UTA

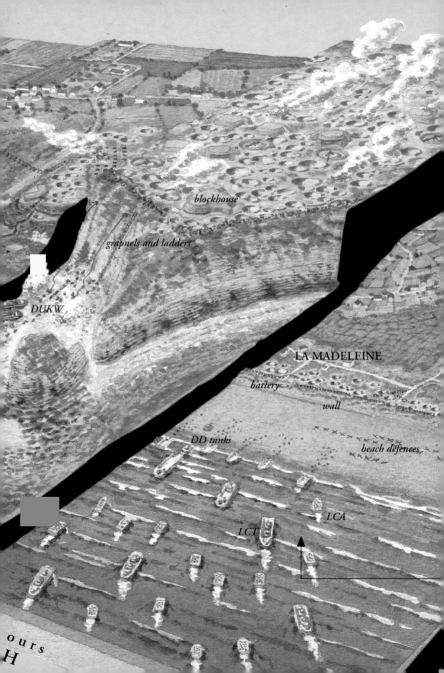

blockhouse

grapnels and ladders

DUKW

LA MADELEINE

battery

wall

DD tanks

beach defences

LCA

LCT

ours

H

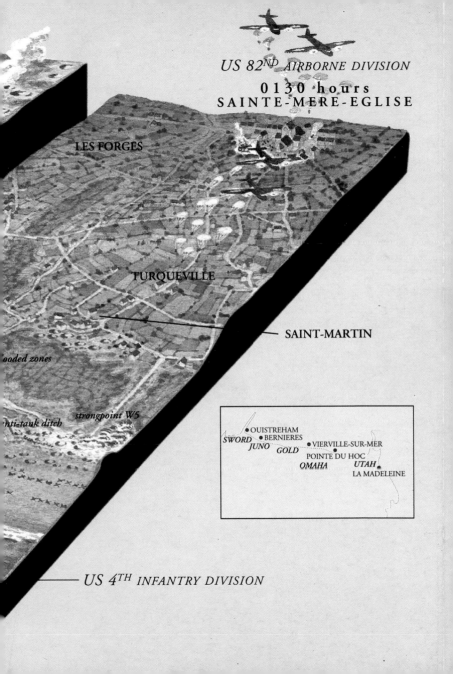

US 82ND AIRBORNE DIVISION

0130 hours
SAINTE-MERE-EGLISE

LES FORGES

TURQUEVILLE

SAINT-MARTIN

flooded zones

anti-tank ditch   *strongpoint W5*

SWORD • OUISTREHAM
• BERNIERES
JUNO   GOLD   • VIERVILLE-SUR-MER
POINTE DU HOC
OMAHA   UTAH
LA MADELEINE

US 4TH INFANTRY DIVISION

Il faut sans délai vous éloigner, avec votre famille, <u>pendant quelques jours</u>, de la zone de danger où vous vous trouvez.

N'encombrez pas les routes.   Dispersez-vous dans la campagne, autant que possible.

PARTEZ SUR LE CHAMP !
VOUS N'AVEZ PAS UNE MINUTE A PERDRE !

Left: General Eisenhower's message to the French inhabitants of the coastal villages of Normandy.

The actual landing was spearheaded by two squadrons of DD tanks which had been successfully launched three kilometres offshore in sheltered water. As they lumbered on to the beach they dropped their rubber 'skirts', and opened fire on the surprised Germans. Behind them the first waves of the US 4th Infantry Division were landed at low tide, well below the beach obstacles. Although the soldiers had to cross more than 500 metres to reach the dunes, return fire was only sporadic. As they and the tanks cleared out the enemy bunkers, teams of engineers landed and started to create paths through the obstacles before the rising tide covered them.

The original landing was quickly reinforced as tanks and artillery arrived together with another regiment of infantry. The infantry soon began to move off across the

Below: from the bridge of the US cruiser Augusta Rear-Admiral Alan Kirk, the naval task force commander (left), General Omar Bradley, commander of the American assault units (in glasses), Brigadier-General William Kean and Rear-Admiral Arthur Struble (with binoculars) watch as events unfold on Utah and Omaha beaches on D-Day.

ATTACK ATTACK ATTACK

Once the beachhead had been established and the engineers had blown passages through the obstacles on the shore, tank landing ships were able to unload their cargo directly on to the beaches. Many, however, were disabled by enemy fire, and their wrecks added to the chaos along the shore. As more and more landing craft arrived, all types of vehicles that were unable to move off remained jammed there. The hero of Utah Beach was Brigadier General Theodore Roosevelt, who, at the age of fifty-seven, calmly directed the traffic.

Left: an American propaganda poster.

causeways over the flooded lagoon, and by 1300 hours, had linked up with the US 101st Airborne Division. By nightfall a solid bridgehead had been established and was being held against uncoordinated German attacks.

By far the worst problem was the congestion on the beach, owing to the restricted exits. As succeeding waves of infantry and armour landed, they had to be moved off as quickly as possible into the firing line to make room for the supplies and heavy equipment that followed.

American forces meet resistance at Omaha Beach

Omaha Beach is about five kilometres in length and is overlooked by high cliffs. The only exits are up the steep ravines at each end that lead to villages of solidly built stone houses. Along the beach runs a concrete sea-wall about three metres high, on top of which one can still see the concrete emplacements that housed 88 mm guns. In theory it was a perfect defensive position, but originally it had been held only by German troops from a weak static division.

The assault regiments from the US 1st Infantry Division had a long approach – nearly sixteen kilometres through the storm-lashed seas – and had to attack

Small teams of heroic medical orderlies did their best to care for the many wounded scattered along the shoreline. Often their only protection was to shelter behind a wrecked landing craft. Many other injured men drowned when the tide came in.

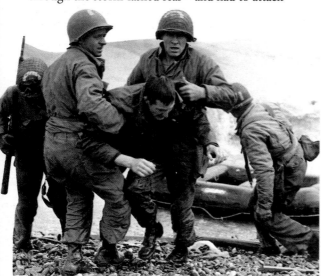

without the promised armoured support. One of the two battalions of DD tanks that were scheduled to be launched about six kilometres offshore considered it too risky. Of the twenty-nine tanks from the other unit, some sank and others were swamped by water pouring over their 'skirts'. Only two reached the beach intact.

Low clouds obscured the bombers' targets and smoke made it difficult for warships to spot theirs, with the result that the defences were both intact and wide-awake as the first wave of landing craft came into view through the haze. The vessels were met by a barrage of shells, mortar bombs and machine-gun fire. Two of the first six craft on one beach sector were sunk, while others ran aground on an offshore sandbank, forcing the men to wade through water up to their shoulders. Many soldiers were shot and many drowned. Small groups of wet, desperate men huddled behind the cover of the sea-wall. On some sectors, other small units did manage to get off the beach but all pretence of cohesion had been abandoned. As successive waves of men and equipment poured into the killing field of Omaha Beach, it was clogged by vehicles that were unable to move. So bad were the conditions that at 0915 hours, General Bradley seriously considered abandoning the landing and rerouting the remaining men through a British beach.

A dead GI lies amid the debris of Omaha Beach, while others run for cover. Within minutes, all semblance of cohesion had been lost. The enemy poured down a hail of mortar and machine-gun fire on the exposed attackers. It was known to Allied intelligence that a veteran German unit, the mobile 352nd Division, had been moved north from Saint-Lô towards the coast, but for some reason this information was not acted upon, with nearly disastrous results. 'As the morning lengthened, my worries deepened...From [the] messages we could piece together only an incoherent account of sinkings, swampings, heavy enemy fire, and chaos on the beaches.' Omar N. Bradley *A Soldier's Story*, 1951

It was sheer courage and the basic survival instinct on the part of individuals and small groups of men that saved the day. Colonel Taylor, the commander of the US 16th Infantry Regiment is reported to have said: 'Two kinds of people are staying on this beach, the dead and those who are going to die – now let's get the hell out of here.' By early afternoon, more tanks had been landed directly on to the beach, but the exits were still open only to men on foot, who had to pick their way through the extensive minefields in single file. By nightfall the US 1st Infantry Division had gained a tenuous hold on the road that ran inland behind

FINAL MOR

San Fran

INVA

NING EDITION

risco Chronicle

SION!

the beach and vehicles were starting to move through the exits. The fact that the Big Red One (the nickname for the US 1st Infantry Division) was not defeated demonstrates the determination and bravery of American troops in Normandy.

Immediately following their landing on Omaha Beach, a team of US Rangers – soldiers specially trained for close-range fighting – attacked the heavy coastal battery at the Pointe du Hoc. Situated on top of high cliffs, and splitting the area between Omaha and Utah beaches, the big German guns at the Pointe were well positioned to fire at both beaches. The Rangers had to scale the cliffs, while Germans threw grenades and fired at them from above. Those who made it to the top engaged in bitter hand-to-hand combat around the strongpoint, only to discover the guns had been moved from the bunkers to a spot further inland. Constantly counter-attacked, the 130 men managed to hold the position through the night.

Gold Beach

Gold Beach, the most westerly beach assigned to the British assault force, extended between the coastal villages of Asnelles and La Rivière. It was the responsibility of the 50th Northumbrian Division and the 8th Armoured Brigade. Attached to them was 47 Royal Marine Commando whose job was to seize Arromanches as a base for the Mulberry harbour.

The US 2nd Ranger Battalion was given the task of scaling the 30-metre high cliffs and eliminating the strong German battery in the concrete bunkers. The six 155 mm howitzers could have fired on Omaha Beach with deadly effect. After a preliminary bombing raid, at 0430 hours, two companies landed on the rocks at the base of the cliffs. In an action reminiscent of a medieval attack on a castle, the Rangers fired rocket-propelled hooks attached to ropes. As the men started to climb, the Germans tried to cut the ropes and dropped grenades on the attackers' heads. Meanwhile, a US destroyer fired at the enemy from close range. One by one the surviving Rangers reached the top only to discover that there were no guns in the bunkers after all. They had been moved to a nearby open field. Owing to the delay in extending the Omaha beachhead, the Rangers had to hold out for two days before the ninety survivors were relieved.

Above: the announcement of the invasion that appeared in the *San Francisco Chronicle* on 6 June 1944.

The weather at the launch site was appalling and it was decided not to launch the DD tanks out to sea, but rather to land them directly behind the infantry. The first waves managed to land clear of the beach obstacles, but the stiff wind buffeting the tide meant that they became obscured more quickly than expected. Successive waves of landing craft had to pick a passage through

Two representations (above and below) of the landing of British troops on Juno Beach.

them and many vessels were damaged in the process. The battle of Gold Beach, however, was won by the specialist armour that landed ahead of the infantry to deal with the defences. By the afternoon the British troops were already marching inland towards Bayeux, and Arromanches had been secured.

Juno Beach

Near the small fishing port of Courseulles-sur-Mer, Juno Beach was assigned to the men of the Canadian 3rd Division, who were thirsting to avenge their losses at Dieppe in 1942. The main problem at Juno was the presence of offshore reefs, which meant that the assault wave would have to land when the rising tide had already covered most of the obstacles.

Since the engineers were unable to clear paths through the underwater obstacles, many of the first landing craft were blown up by mines. In spite of the aerial bombardment, there were enough Germans holed up in the houses along the sea front to fire on to the beaches as the Canadians dashed for cover. The arrival of specialist armour was also delayed on many sectors. This delay hindered the clearing of the beach exits, which in turn led to congestion on the beaches. As wave after wave of vehicles and tanks were landed, they had to pick their way through the wrecked landing craft along the high-tide mark.

The North Shore Regiment had a hard fight at Saint-Aubin where they had to prise the Germans out of the underground passages of a strongpoint. Yet other units backed by tanks pressed inland and by evening a solid bridgehead – linking the Canadians with the British XXX Corps from Gold Beach – had been established.

Sword Beach

Sword Beach, the most easterly of the British landing beaches, was to be assaulted by the 3rd Division and its supporting units, including a force of French Commandos

Two types of obstacles (below) placed on the beaches by Rommel's troops. In the foreground is an anti-tank mine fixed to the top of a metal post, designed to detonate if hit by landing craft. In the background is a tetrahedron or 'hedgehog' for ripping open the thin skins of boats. On all the beaches, teams of engineers with the task of blowing lanes through the obstacles were among the first to land. They suffered severe casualties.

serving with the Lord Lovat's 1st Commando Brigade. The Commandos were to clear a way through the town of Ouistreham and then meet the hard-pressed troops of the British 6th Airborne Division at the Orne bridgehead. At Ouistreham the assaulting troops were faced by a solid line of sea-front villas – even a casino that the Germans had turned into a fortress.

After a massive preliminary bombardment, the heaviest on any of the beaches that day, the DD tanks were launched. In spite of the heavy seas, most of them reached the shore, closely followed by the LCTs loaded with the specialist armoured vehicles. On their heels came the infantry, who managed to clear the shore line and then stormed the houses one by one. Soon the first groups of grey-clad German prisoners were stumbling back towards the shore. As the tide rose, the strip of beach became so congested that further landings had to be halted until the specialist armour and the engineers could clear the exits.

The Commandos made short work of the fortified casino and quickly cleared the town of Ouistreham. Lord Lovat and his men then broke out into open country and began their march towards the bridges over the Orne and the canal. They faced light opposition, but became entangled at the bridgehead in the battle between the 6th Airborne and the 21st Panzer Division.

The Scottish Brigadier Lord Lovat led the 1st Commando Brigade ashore at Ouistreham. Lovat was wounded on 12 June in the bridgehead east of the Orne River and evacuated to hospital.

The first German prisoners being marched along the beach at Bernières to board the empty landing craft that would take them back to England.

Consolidation and counter-attacks

By midday Hitler's Atlantic Wall had been breached, although the Allies' toehold was still precarious, especially at Omaha Beach. The landing of the follow-up units on the various beaches was severely hampered

The French detachment of commander Philippe Kieffer (above) was formed of two troops of 125 men incorporated in 4 Commando. Many people escaped from France by secretly boarding Breton fishing boats. Others came from French territories in West Africa. The British officer in charge of the Commando described them as 'stubborn soldiers, confident of their own strength, quick in action and really very courageous'.

by both the weather and the lack of exits for such heavy traffic. Enemy interference from the sea had been negligible and the Luftwaffe failed to put in an appearance. What German sorties were made were mainly to the north, where valuable flying hours were consumed in hunting for the non-existent deception convoys.

As a direct result of their tangled chain of command, the Germans lost the initiative at the vital moment. Rommel, who might have been able to galvanize the troops, did not return from Germany until late in the afternoon of D-Day. Von Runstedt remained convinced that the landings in Normandy were a diversion and that

By the evening of D-Day the Americans had managed to consolidate a slender bridgehead inland from Omaha Beach (above), which remained congested with vehicles and wreckage, while follow-up units remained at sea.

The fortuitous absence of Rommel (left) added to the confusion in the tangled German chain of command. He was told of the invasion by a telephone call late in the morning to his home in Germany. He left immediately but did not reach his headquarters until the late afternoon. Rommel's beach obstacles had failed to hinder the landings, and he lacked the mobile reserves to defeat the Allies before they could consolidate a bridgehead.

the main assault would come later in the Calais area, a view shared by the Wehrmacht (German army) high command. Although there were two armoured divisions within striking distance of Normandy, Panzer Lehr Division and the 12th SS (*Schutzstaffel* or elite corps) Panzer Division Hitler Jugend, neither could be moved without the permission of Hitler, who was fast asleep at his villa in Berchtesgaden in southeastern Bavaria. It was midday before he became aware of the situation and reluctantly gave permission for the two divisions to move. When they did so in the late afternoon, they were harried by the Allied fighter-bombers.

A pair of well-camouflaged Tiger tanks of the 21st Panzer Division parked among the trees (below). The division consisted of only one tank regiment backed by two regiments of Panzergrenadiere, mechanized infantry, and a battalion of assault guns improvised from captured French material. Stationed to the south and east of Caen, it was the only mobile unit capable of a decisive counter-attack. However, Rommel had issued orders that the division was not to intervene in the case of enemy landings without orders from his headquarters. By the end of D-Day, 21st Panzer had lost a quarter of its tanks, but was between the British and Caen.

The one formation that was readily available, the 21st Panzer, commanded by Major-General Edgar Feuchtinger, was largely paralysed by having first received no orders, then contrary ones. Aware of the British 6th Airborne bridgehead, Feuchtinger had decided to mount a general assault, only to be told to concentrate his tanks on the other side of the Orne. It was not until late afternoon that his forces were in a position to check the belated British advance from Sword Beach trying to arrive at Caen. A few German tanks did reach the coast in the gap between Sword Beach and Juno Beach, but not in sufficient numbers to cause serious disruption. By the end of the day, the 21st Panzer Division had lost a quarter of its armoured strength but was still deployed to bar the way into Caen.

Convinced that the weather was too bad for an Allied landing, Major-General Feuchtinger (above) was not in Normandy on the night of 5 June.

There was an enormous sense of relief back at the various headquarters in England that losses had not been as heavy as expected. General Eisenhower, powerless to intervene, had to content himself with reading the

IT'S UP TO

US TO LET 'EM HAVE IT!

reports as they came in to Southwick House. When news came of the disaster at Omaha Beach, the terrible strain he was under became obvious to those with him.

By the evening of D-Day, the Allies had managed to land 130,000 soldiers across the beaches, plus 22,000 men dropped by air. The entire assault force had suffered some only 8600 casualties. This was an incredible achievement, though few of the immediate D-Day objectives had actually been achieved. The British 3rd Division had failed to take Caen and the Canadians had been unable to capture the airfield at Carpiquet. The American troops who had landed on Utah Beach had pushed several miles inland to link up with the hard-pressed airborne divisions, but the situation at Omaha Beach, where the bridgehead was in places less than a kilometre deep, was causing concern. Before any attempt could be made to cut off Cherbourg – thereby isolating the German army on Contentin Peninsula – the road junction and bridges at Carentan had to be captured and the two American bridgeheads united into a solid front.

Carpiquet airfield, to the west of Caen, remained firmly in German hands on the evening of D-Day. Stiff resistance from the German 716th Infantry Division had stopped the Canadians well short of their objective. It took weeks of bitter fighting before the Allies were able to capture the cratered ruins.

The 'Overlord' embroidery

Commissioned by Lord Dulverton as a tribute to those involved in the Normandy landings, the 'Overlord' embroidery was made by twenty women from the Royal School of Needlework between 1968 and 1973. The embroidery, which is kept in the D-Day Museum in Portsmouth, consists of thirty-four panels, measuring eighty-two metres in total. It is a permanent reminder to all nations of the importance of liberty and democracy. Opposite: the Allies head for Normandy on the evening of 5 June 1944. Following pages: in the early morning of 6 June the fighter-bombers and the fleet start attacking the enemy defences; the first men set foot on the beaches; the first casualties; the Germans are thrown into panic; the villages of Normandy in ruins. The use of materials from real uniforms gives this work of craftsmanship a strong dramatic tone.

Although not all the initial objectives had been reached, 'Operation Neptune' was a success, with far fewer casualties than had been expected. The next phase of 'Overlord' was to build up sufficient forces to defeat the German army in Normandy and then to head east towards the Seine. This stage of the campaign was really a race between the two sides.

CHAPTER 4
CONSOLIDATION

American troops from the 29th Infantry Division (left) move into the battered ruins of Saint-Lô on 18 July 1944.

Right: the German generals – Kurt Meyer (left), the commander of the 36th SS Panzergrenadier Regiment, Fritz Witt (centre), the commander of the 12th SS Panzer Division, and Max Wünsche (right), commander of the 12th SS Panzer Regiment.

General Montgomery knew he had to seize sufficient
territory to form an operating base, while at the same
time bringing fresh divisions ashore and stockpiling
the required supplies, ammunition, vehicles and fuel.
If he could do this more quickly than the Germans
could bring in reinforcements, then he would win
the battle. Air superiority was crucial, and by
D+1 (the day following D-Day),
British and American fighter-bombers
were operating from improvised air-
strips in Normandy. Their ability
to hinder the movement of
German reinforcements in
daylight was one of the key
factors in the eventual victory.
The one factor over which
Montgomery had no
control, however, was the
weather, which affected
all incoming shipments.
Montgomery's small
tactical headquarters
had left for Normandy on
the morning of 6 June and
he himself embarked on a
destroyer that evening.

SMA

The following morning he cruised along the beaches and conferred with General Bradley, who was also patrolling the beaches on board the US cruiser *Augusta*. He ordered Bradley to concentrate on joining his two lodgment areas. Lieutenant-General Miles Dempsey, commander of the British Second Army, was instructed to surround Caen by advancing on each side of the city. Bayeux was the first large town to be captured early on the morning of D+1 and thus British forces now controlled the main east–west road. But a low cloud restricted flying and imposed a severe delay on the landing of further troops and supplies.

Thanks to the convincing work of Allied double agents, the German high command still resolutely believed that the landings in Normandy were a feint and refused to move any Fifteenth Army units south of the Seine. Rommel therefore had to make do with his own

SHING AHEAD!

Nazis Say We're 10 Miles In;

reserves and started to bring up the 12th SS Panzer Division Hitler Jugend, but such was the shortage of petrol that it arrived piecemeal and had to be thrown into the battle around Caen which was being fought by the 21st Panzer Division. Thus the chance of a heavy armoured counter-attack was lost by then as the British were well dug-in. The only other division within striking distance was Panzer Lehr, which attempted to move in daylight and suffered heavy losses from Allied fighter-bombers. The movement of German infantry reserves from Brittany was equally hampered by lack of petrol and chaotic conditions on the railway system. Rommel's troops were fighting in three places at once – at Caen, at Bayeux (which they were trying to recapture) and at the junction of the American bridgeheads.

British troops marching into Bayeux on 7 June 1944 (opposite above).

Opposite: General Bernard Montgomery (centre) in Normandy with General Omar Bradley (left), the commander of the US First Army, and General Miles Dempsey (right), who headed the British Second Army. Dempsey's unassuming manner meant he was always overshadowed by his superior.

Above: one of the fanatical young soldiers of the 12th SS Panzer Division.

The British front

Meanwhile, just over three kilometres to the west of Caen, Canadian efforts to capture the airfield at Carpiquet were stalled by bitter resistance from the 12th SS Panzer Division. A British Commando unit captured the small harbour of Port-en-Bessin and was thus able to link up with the Americans in the Omaha bridgehead. The US V Corps had made an astonishing recovery after its disastrous landing on Omaha Beach and on the morning of 9 June Montgomery was able to order Bradley to move the corps southwards towards Coutances and Saint-Lô to cover Dempsey's flank. Within two days the Allies had enlarged the area under their control to a depth of more than twenty kilometres. At the same time, the US 101st Airborne Division was

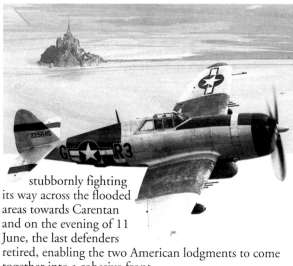

stubbornly fighting its way across the flooded areas towards Carentan and on the evening of 11 June, the last defenders retired, enabling the two American lodgments to come together into a cohesive front.

Aircraft such as this American P47 Thunderbolt (left) flying near Mont Saint-Michel and the British Typhoons were greatly feared by the Germans. Unhindered by the Luftwaffe, they swept down on the unprotected enemy fortifications, shooting at anything that moved. The Germans, who called them 'Jabos', were forced to move their troops at night.

Montgomery's intention was for Bradley's men to head south to cut off the Cherbourg peninsula and then move west to capture the port. The British and Canadians would help by detaining the German armour around Caen. The panzer divisions were to be trapped in a vast pincer movement either side of the city and an airborne division was to demolish their rear. The Allies

As German resistance around the city of Caen stiffened, British troops found themselves fighting the Germans over ruined dwellings – such as this burning farmhouse (left) – which were easily turned into strongpoints.

On 14 June General Charles de Gaulle was finally permitted to set foot in liberated France. Escorted by military police, he made a speech in Bayeux, where he was greeted by crowds of people and quickly hustled away. After a brief meeting with General Montgomery, de Gaulle returned to England, much to the relief of the Allied political and military leaders.

had 16 divisions ashore by 11 June, facing 14 German divisions, but losses had reached 15,000 and supplies were still twenty-four hours behind schedule. Dempsey's army, which had been brought to a standstill by Panzer Lehr blocking the way through Tilly-sur-Seulles, was exhausted. The soldiers found themselves caught in the dense *bocage* – countryside with tall ancient hedgerows between which ran sunken roads – perfect for defence. Tanks were unusable.

By 13 June a temporary stalemate had descended upon the battlefield and Montgomery had to call a halt to his great plans for an envelopment of Caen and an American break-out into Brittany via Saint-Lô. The enemy had managed temporarily to recapture Carentan, and the British 7th Armoured Division, the famous Desert Rats, was unable to claim Villers-Bocage. Yet, Montgomery had succeeded in thwarting a massive counter-stroke by Rommel.

Logistics: the installation of the Mulberry harbours

The Allies had enough problems of their own, owing to the slow build-up of forces and a shortage of artillery ammunition. The first components of the Mulberry harbours had arrived in Normandy on D+1; by 18 June most of the outer caissons for the two harbours were in position and work was underway to install the floating pierheads. In the early hours of 19 June, however, a savage storm sank several sections of the floating roadway that was being towed across the Channel. The tempest, which raged for three whole days, demolished the American Mulberry at Omaha Beach and severely damaged the British one at Arromanches. Hundreds of landing craft were stranded on the beaches or sunk

offshore, and unloading came virtually to a halt. Montgomery's plan to attack across the Odon River to keep up the pressure on Rommel had to be abandoned, giving the enemy a chance to rest and regroup.

The Cherbourg campaign

It was in the west of the peninsula, however, that the absence of German armour enabled Major-General Joseph Lawton Collins and his US VII Corps to exploit the situation. One of the best fighting generals of the war, 'Lightning Joe' Collins pushed his untried GIs through the *bocage* in a series of short stabbing moves through the thinly manned German line.

By 18 June the two Mulberry harbours were in position and operating around the clock. However, a fierce storm caused severe damage – the outer lines of the massive concrete caissons were breached by the waves, the floating roadways were torn apart and flung on to the beaches, and ships broke their moorings and sank. Although the harbour at Arromanches was repaired, the one at Omaha Beach had to be abandoned. In this way the build-up of supplies was delayed.

An aerial view of the Mulberry harbour at Saint-Laurent (left), at the eastern end of Omaha Beach. In the foreground is the end of the outer wall of Phoenix caissons forming the breakwater, inside which merchant ships and landing craft were anchored. Three of the Spud floating pierheads were joined to the shore by Whale floating roadways that were strong enough to carry tanks and trucks.

An American armoured car on a Whale roadway, heading for the shore after unloading (opposite). The roadways were anchored to the beaches after the high tide mark, from where the engineers had bulldozed exit roads into the interior. The ready assembled roadways were towed across the Channel in sections. On arrival they were bolted together and joined up to the pierheads. Floating pontoons supported lengths of steel roadway.

Early on the morning of 18 June, the advance units of the US 9th Infantry Division marched into the tiny seaside village of Barneville on the west coast of the Cotentin Peninsula, opposite Utah Beach. The entire peninsula was thus successfully cut off and the remaining German forces surrounded. The following morning, giving the Germans no chance to react, Collins had three

YANKS CH

divisions ready to move north, and, with no preliminary artillery bombardment, the US 4th Infantry Division caught the enemy by surprise in Montebourg, on the southeastern coast of the peninsula. By the evening of 24 June the Americans, moving rapidly, were on the heights overlooking Cherbourg.

Collins concentrated his three divisions on the port, using reconnaissance units to watch his flanks, and made extensive use of naval artillery and fighter-bombers to pin down the defenders. His infantry then crept forward and blasted them from bunker to bunker. The German garrison commander, General von Schlieben, issued old French rifles to cooks and supplymen, obeying Hitler's order that the harbour and city had to be defended to the last man. By the evening of 26 June the Americans had entered Cherbourg and had managed to capture von Schlieben, although the

General Joseph Lawton Collins – 'Lightning Joe' – the charismatic commander of the US VII Corps.

RGE AT HEART OF CHERBOURG

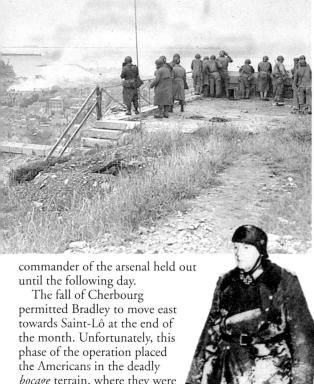

As Cherbourg was the only port in Normandy capable of berthing the largest ocean-going ships, its capture was of vital importance to the Allies. Well fortified by the Germans, it could only be approached via narrow defiles leading down from the surrounding hills. By cutting the peninsula in half on 18 June, 30,000 Germans were trapped as the Americans turned west towards Cherbourg. In bitter fighting the enemy was slowly forced back inside the perimeter of the fortress. Once the American troops had taken the heights above the town on 24 June (above, the Fort du Roule), the fate of the fortress was sealed, despite Hitler's orders. General Karl-Wilhelm von Schlieben (left), the garrison commander, surrendered. Demolition engineers had done a thorough job, so it was to be several weeks before the port could be opened for Allied use.

A German Panzer Mark IV tank (opposite top) moving up to the front.

commander of the arsenal held out until the following day.

The fall of Cherbourg permitted Bradley to move east towards Saint-Lô at the end of the month. Unfortunately, this phase of the operation placed the Americans in the deadly *bocage* terrain, where they were to face severe losses until they could gain adequate footing for a break-out. While Bradley regrouped and laid down stocks of ammunition, Montgomery planned to break out across the Odon River to the west of Caen, thus keeping Rommel's panzer divisions off balance and away from the Americans.

'Operation Epsom' – the drive on Caen

General Sir Richard O'Connor (left), who commanded the British VIII Corps in Normandy.

Although Hitler and his entourage, misled by Allied deception and the incompetence of their own intelligence services, still maintained that the Allies planned to make another landing in the Pas-de-Calais, Rommel was reluctantly given some reinforcements. By the end of June he had eight panzer divisions in Normandy, two of which had been stripped from the eastern front. However, there were still more divisions guarding the coast north of the Seine than fighting the Allies in the bridgehead. Rommel's overall aim was to concentrate his armour and by attacking the British in the Bayeux area, to split the British from the Americans and force them to a second Dunkirk.

Montgomery, in his headquarters between Bayeux and Caen, had his own plans. His scheme had been to draw the enemy's attention away from Cherbourg by forcing them into battle at Caen. The purpose was more than diversionary, however, as its capture – in conjunction with Cherbourg's – would ideally position the Allies for the break-out towards the Seine. The storm, however, had caused him a temporary loss of the initiative and given his adversary the chance to build up his defences. Through Allied 'Ultra' intelligence (the decoding of the German military messages) Montgomery was fully aware of the moves of panzer reinforcements into the battle area. Yet he was unable to attack until more forces had landed. These included the British VIII Corps commanded by the veteran of the North African campaign General O'Connor. Captured by the Italians, he escaped in time to be selected to command a corps for the Normandy campaign.

After the dismal failure to capture Villers-Bocage, Montgomery found his room for manoeuvre was strictly

A German 'Enigma' coding machine (above) consisted of a keyboard and rotating drums that could scramble messages.

limited in that he could not attack Caen frontally. His original intention had been to attack east of the city out of the Orne bridgehead – which had been seized by the airborne forces on D-Day itself – and then to move south to control the Falaise plain. There he hoped to trap the enemy in a 'pocket' formed by the Canadian First Army from the north, the US Third Army from the south and the US First Army from the west. There, however, space was strictly limited and an army corps would not have had enough room to deploy. With strong forces on the high ground around Villers-Bocage to the west of Caen, the enemy was in control of that area, which left only the relatively favourable countryside in the centre of Dempsey's front leading down to the Odon River, a tributary of the Orne. Beyond the river there was open farmland dominated by one of the few pieces of high ground in the area, Hill 112, and then the way would be clear to cross the Orne towards the Falaise plain. For 'Operation Epsom' Montgomery planned to use the two infantry and one armoured division of VIII Corps on a front six kilometres wide, backed by

The first major tank battle in Normandy took place at Aunay-sur-Odon (below) where British forces were pitted against all the available German tanks. At the same time it was a classic infantry battle as the foot-soldiers had to dislodge the enemy from the houses built from stone and advance across the open corn fields. The bitter fighting for control of Hill 112 recalled the trench warfare of the First World War.

a massive combination of artillery and tactical air power. The attack was originally scheduled for 22 June, but the continuing bad weather postponed the landing of supplies and everything had to be delayed for three days.

The temporary lull had given the Germans enough time to establish a strong defensive line along the Orne, which was held by the 12th SS Panzer Hitler Jugend, reinforced with units from the 21st Panzer to the east and Panzer Lehr to the west. The Hitler Jugend Division was the toughest of the German units in Normandy, commanded by the legendary Kurt 'Panzer' Meyer and largely made up of fanatical youngsters. When the British attack started behind a massive bombardment, the weather was so bad that the fighter-bombers were grounded. The Scottish 15th Division led the way, but quickly became embroiled in hand-to-hand combat in the stone-built villages along the river. On the right, the XXX Corps was unable to take Rauray, and in spite of an advance of nearly six kilometres, the day ended in a sea of mud and pouring rain.

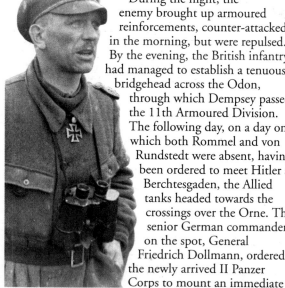

During the night, the enemy brought up armoured reinforcements, counter-attacked in the morning, but were repulsed. By the evening, the British infantry had managed to establish a tenuous bridgehead across the Odon, through which Dempsey passed the 11th Armoured Division. The following day, on a day on which both Rommel and von Rundstedt were absent, having been ordered to meet Hitler at Berchtesgaden, the Allied tanks headed towards the crossings over the Orne. The senior German commander on the spot, General Friedrich Dollmann, ordered the newly arrived II Panzer Corps to mount an immediate

German General Kurt 'Panzer' Meyer (left), who took command of the 12th SS Panzer Division Hitler Jugend on 16 June after General Fritz Witt was killed. Many of his troops were only seventeen years old, but, despite their age, they proved to be formidable opponents.

General Friedrich Dollmann (above), commander of the German Seventh Army, was responsible for the defence of Normandy and Brittany. Caught up in the tangled German chain of command, he was unable to exert any decisive influence on the battle on D-Day. On the afternoon of 6 June von Rundstedt gave him orders to clear the beachhead by that evening. By that time, however, the battle was lost. Demoralized by the fall of Cherbourg, he committed suicide.

counter-attack, and then committed suicide that evening. The next day, on 29 June, was a day of confusion on both sides. The British 11th Armoured Division managed to capture Hill 112, but two divisions of the II Panzer Corps – the 9th and 10th – attacked from the west. The British infantry inflicted a crushing defeat on them, but Dempsey, mistakenly thinking that the enemy might mount an even heavier attack, pulled his 11th Armoured back over the Odon because he was worried about the vulnerability of his bridgehead.

This removal of armour enabled the Germans to retake Hill 112 and the fighting degenerated into small vicious actions reminiscent of trench warfare during the First World War. Concerned by the rapidly mounting

German armour (left) sheltering under trees. It was camouflaged with branches to avoid observation from the air. Only the élite panzer divisions of the German army were motorized. The infantry marched on foot, and the bulk of its transport and artillery was horse-drawn. Those vehicles they did have suffered from constant shortages of petrol.

Although their houses had been left in ruins from the Allied bombardment, the citizens of Normandy were still able to greet the Allied troops warmly. Left: a couple of farmers from the Saint-Lô area drink calvados with American soldiers.

losses, especially among the infantry, Montgomery was forced to terminate 'Epsom' on 30 June. According to the VIII Corps war diary, the three divisions involved suffered more than 4000 casualties, wounded and missing during the five-day battle. The Germans had suffered equally badly of course, but that could not disguise the fact that 'Epsom' had been yet another costly failure. Montgomery had a complete British corps as well as another Canadian one ready to land at Normandy, but the failure to expand the bridgehead meant that he had nowhere to put them. The whole of the rear area of the Second Army was simply choked with supplies and vehicles, with more piling up daily on the beaches as the weather began to improve.

The Americans in the *bocage*

While the British and Canadians were forced on to the defensive, Bradley prepared for his delayed offensive. This plan entailed an advance on a broad front with the entire US First Army, to capture the Saint-Lô-Périers road, before breaking out into Brittany. On paper the Americans had a distinct advantage, with four army corps ranged against only six German divisions, several of which were

A Frenchman reads the latest news in one of the Vichy-controlled papers. Many of his countrymen, however, relied on the BBC for accurate information about the state of the war.

little more than regimental-strength battle groups, along a seventy-kilometre front, but the terrain was distinctly unfavourable. There were few roads leading to the east and the enemy remained in firm control of Saint-Lô itself, which was the hub of the entire highway network in the area. Several flooded and marshy river valleys lay in the line of advance, and German troops were well positioned on the high ground to the east around La Haye-du-Puits.

An American infantry platoon (above) moves along a typically small road in the *bocage* near Saint-Lô. The thick hedgerows, many of them centuries old, formed perfect defensive positions and were solid enough to stop tanks. A handful of men with grenades and anti-tank rockets could hold up a battalion. It took a month of bitter fighting before the Americans were in a position to break out of the confines of the *bocage*. The Germans brought in tough veteran airborne troops to defend the area around Saint-Lô.

But once again an Allied offensive backed by massive firepower from artillery and aircraft was hindered by stubborn German defence from hedgerow to hedgerow. Although the German troops suffered appalling casualty rates, their morale did not appear to falter as they obeyed their Führer's order to defend every square metre of ground. Three weeks after the Allied landings, at the beginning of July, von Rundstedt – having failed to thwart the invasion – was replaced by Field-Marshal Gunther von Kluge as supreme commander in the west.

Bradley's offensive got underway on 3 July, with the US VIII Corps, which was already established on firm ground across the marshy Douve River in the peninsula's centre, sending four divisions eastwards to attack in the direction of La-Haye-du-Puits and the Forêt de Monte Castre. They encountered extremely stubborn resistance from veteran airborne troops and although they managed to take the town on 8 June, the enemy was still in possession of the surrounding hills. In the centre, the VII Corps failed to make any significant progress down the Carentan–Périers road, and by 10 July, the entire offensive was stalled.

The failure to capture Caen

Montgomery was becoming increasingly frustrated by the inability of the British and Canadians to make any

Often the unsung heroes of war, the medical services tended both their own men and the enemy's wounded. The unit doctors, who had to work under shell fire, set up their aid stations in farmhouses just behind the front line. Those that could be saved were then evacuated in trucks (above) to the field hospitals, and from there to England.

At the beginning of July the 12th SS Panzer Division Hitler Jugend was still in control of the Carpiquet area. In support of the main assault on Caen, the Canadian 3rd Division was ordered to capture Carpiquet. Supported by the guns of the battleship HMS *Rodney*, an infantry brigade and the tanks of the Port Garry Horse Regiment advanced, dislodging the German troops from the village. The survivors, however, retreated to the airfield itself, where they dug in and defended themselves, building by building. Rocket-firing Typhoon aircraft swooped down and flame-thrower tanks rumbled into the barracks. After four days of bitter fighting, the Canadians were masters of the ruins. To the west, other Canadian units were also engaged with the 12th SS Panzer Division, struggling to clear the villages between the airfield and the city. No longer able to hold the line, Kurt Meyer pulled the remnants of his division back behind the Orne River.

impression in the Caen sector. The city itself no longer had any importance for the Germans in military terms, but Hitler characteristically had ordered that it be defended to the last man. Montgomery, having decided a direct attack would be too costly, had tried to bypass Caen and failed. The airfield at Carpiquet was still firmly in the hands of the Germans, who were stubbornly defending all possible routes towards the more open country of the Falaise plain that the British needed to control if they were to swing north-east towards the Seine crossings and Paris. Montgomery therefore reverted to the tactics of carpet-bombing Caen and then attempting a direct assault to capture the bridges over the Orne in the city centre. A secondary consideration in his general strategy was that pressure on the Germans in the Caen area should be maintained to prevent their transferring armoured divisions to the west

Above: a Messerschmidt 210 airplane destroyed in the Allied bombing of the Carpiquet airfield.

to oppose Bradley. On 3 July, the day the American attack started, the Canadian 3rd Division was ordered to capture Carpiquet airfield, where once again it ran into the 12th SS Panzer. In a vicious two-day battle that cost both sides heavy casualties, the Canadians managed to capture the village and part of the airfield before the attack ground to a halt.

The campaign to capture Caen was due to start on 8 July with an attack by British I Corps. At the last moment Montgomery decided to ask for the support of the Royal Air Force Bomber Command and in the late evening of 7 July heavy aircraft dropped 6000 bombs on the northern part of Caen, turning that fine old Norman city into a heap of rubble. In three days of bitter fighting the

The massive attack by Bomber Command reduced the historic centre of Caen to a field of rubble. British troops then had to struggle against German snipers holed up in the ruins. Only the shells of the magnificent medieval abbey and churches survived. The operation may have freed the actual city, but the enemy was still able to block any move southwards towards Falaise.

infantry struggled through the piles of rubble and bomb craters, taking heavy losses in the process. Eventually the Germans were forced to give ground, but they established themselves on the south bank of the Orne, which runs right through the city centre. Thus Montgomery, contrary to ecstatic press reports issued at the time, had captured only half the city. The vital Bourguébus ridge to the south, which commanded the way to the Falaise plain, remained in enemy hands.

Three British soldiers pose beside a road marker from Caen.

No real gains had been made in terms of territory in which to deploy the troops who were still waiting in England.

Controversy and stalemate

Ever since the war, there has been fierce controversy about the conduct of the fighting in Normandy. As commander of the ground forces, Montgomery was responsible for the actual conduct of operations. Eisenhower, relegated to watching from the sidelines, became increasingly frustrated at what he regarded as slow progress. Eisenhower tended towards a strategy of continuous fighting all along the front, all the time. Montgomery on the other hand liked to fight a set-piece battle and to concentrate force where it could achieve the maximum gains. A strong anti-Montgomery lobby at SHAEF helped to fuel the supreme commander's impatience, and towards the end of June there was a movement to have Montgomery replaced by General Alexander.

While Eisenhower might have liked to have taken personal command in Normandy, this action was precluded by his duties as supreme commander. By the end of June, the Americans in the field were becoming increasingly critical of British slowness, although, in fairness, their own progress had hardly been spectacular. Both sides had failed to appreciate the difficulties of operating in the *bocage*.

By D+30 the situation in Normandy was at a stalemate. The British forces lacked sufficient space for manoeuvre and had an uneven front line on either side

General Eisenhower (far left) with General Bradley (on his right) paid many visits to Normandy. His SHAEF headquarters, which consisted of 15,000 people, was still located in England, and did not move to Granville in Normandy until mid-August. Deeply frustrated by what he saw as lack of progress, he listened to staff officers in his own headquarters who began to be openly critical of Montgomery. Although it was only a question of time before the Germans were defeated, the Allies were trapped both by the difficult terrain and logistical problems.

The ruined towns and villages (left) bore witness to the terrible price paid by the Normans for the liberation of their country.

Although Montgomery (below) continued to be optimistic, the press was beginning to complain about the lack of progress. His strategy of drawing the German armoured forces on to the British front around Caen had worked, but the Americans were still caught up in the *bocage*. Although they had been severely mauled, the Germans showed no signs of collapse.

of Caen. The Americans were still trapped in difficult terrain from which they had to extricate themselves before they could attempt to break out towards Brittany through the Avranches gap. The main factor in their favour was the continued success of 'Operation Fortitude', the deception campaign. Still believing that the 'real' invasion at the Pas-de-Calais was imminent, the German High Command refused to release troops from north of the Seine. This made it impossible for Rommel to gather a large enough force to mount a credible counter-attack.

At the time, Montgomery was claiming that everything was still going according to his master plan, but many other high-ranking Allied officers began to worry about the Allied forces becoming cut off in Normandy. Recognizing that they had inflicted terrible casualties on the enemy, Eisenhower was confident that it was only a question of time before German resistance would snap. But where?

At the beginning of July 1944 Montgomery was under intense pressure to bring the campaign in Normandy to a victorious end. Yet he still found himself constantly hampered by the enemy's defensive tactics and the poor weather. Stalemate had been reached and he had to produce a result – quickly.

CHAPTER 5

BREAK-OUT

The Allied commanders (left) in early August, just before the final break-out that was to end the campaign in Normandy. From left to right: General Patton, commander of the US Third Army, General Bradley, commander of the US 12th Army Group, and – now his equal rather than his superior – General Montgomery, commander of the 21st Army Group.

German soldiers (right) in Villers-Bocage.

Dempsey was ordered first to clear the Germans out of the southern suburbs of Caen and then to attack over the Orne towards Thury-Harcourt, nineteen kilometres to the south. Three armoured divisions were to be pulled out of line and assembled as a separate corps. Until then, tanks had had little effect on the fighting in Normandy, being of little use in the *bocage*, and the brunt of the losses had been borne by the infantry.

Bradley, meanwhile, was to fight his way eastwards and, when Avranches was reached, to push one corps into Brittany while rest of the army headed southeast. Oddly enough, there was no mention yet of Patton's Third Army, which was waiting in the wings to exploit a break-out.

Bradley decided on a concentrated strike on a narrow front instead of slugging it out all along the line. For what became known as 'Operation Cobra', he chose the line of the Saint-Lô–Périers–Lessay road. His intention was to launch a massive air bombardment just prior to an all-out attack by the VIII Corps.

Dempsey was unhappy about the idea of continuing the futile infantry battles along the Odon, and instead came up with what he considered a better solution, known as 'Operation Goodwood'. His plan was to launch the three armoured divisions to the east of Caen out of the airborne bridgehead captured on D-Day, which had hardly been expanded. The tanks were to capture the all-important Bourguébus ridge, which acted as the gateway to the road from Caen to Falaise. Once the enemy was locked in battle to the east, the rest of the Second Army would launch operations to the west of Caen, thus catching any German response off-guard.

General Miles Dempsey (left), commander of the British Second Army, was given the task of breaking the stalemate by clearing the Germans out of the southern suburbs of Caen. At the same time he had to divert the enemy panzer divisions from the American front, where General Bradley was still struggling to clear the *bocage*.

'Operation Goodwood'

Dempsey planned to launch a heavy air bombardment at the beginning of the operation and to support his forces with naval gunfire. As his comments at the time show, he was optimistic and was contemplating exploitation towards Falaise, on the assumption that the German resistance would crumble. Unknown to him, however, the Germans knew that the British were coming, had no intention of giving up and had built up a series of strong defensive positions well equipped with anti-tank guns. They had a number of heavy Tiger tanks and plenty of the deadly 88 mm guns that could penetrate the lightly armoured Allied tanks. Ironically, the day before

American troops (left) advance in the Saint-Lô area about 20 July 1944. The relatively inexperienced American units quickly developed into a strong fighting force. According to Montgomery's strategy, the Americans would force the issue by breaking out to the south of the Cotentin Peninsula, while the German armour was engaged against the British around Caen. General Bradley had the men and the equipment to do the job, but many of his units were still held up by determined German defenders in the *bocage* and poor weather conditions hindered the use of air power.

The British Second Army (left) take part in a German ambush near Tracy-Bocage during 'Operation Goodwood'. The chosen area near Caen was extremely restricted, allowing only limited space for the three armoured divisions to assemble. They had to advance down a narrow corridor of land which was crossed by two railway embankments. Furthermore, the enemy had excellent observation posts in the huge steelworks at Colombelles, in the eastern suburbs of Caen, and in the high ground to the south.

'Goodwood' was finally mounted, on 17 July, Rommel was severely wounded when his staff car was attacked by a fighter aircraft. He took no further part in the Normandy campaign and was replaced by von Kluge.

Early on the morning of 18 July, thousands of tons of bombs rained down on the Germans, saturating the area around Bourguébus and their exit routes. In theory, none of the enemy should have survived – but enough men did. The 11th Armoured Division, commanded by General Roberts led the way, but soon ran into difficulties owing to a flaw in the planning that ordered him to use his infantry to clear German strongpoints in a number of villages, instead of advancing with the tanks. Complicating matters was the massive traffic jam that formed around the bridges over the canal and the Orne, which were swamped by the vehicles from the 7th Armoured and the Guards Armoured Divisions.

As the lead units of Roberts' division stormed towards Bourguébus, they were engaged by a battle group of the 21st Panzer Division in the village of Cagny. Sixteen British tanks were destroyed immediately. By midday the advance had shuddered to a halt and the 7th Armoured Division still had not crossed the start line. The Guards Armoured Division was pinned down by the fire from Cagny, and General O'Connor began to realize that he had lost the initiative. Montgomery, however, was proclaiming a major victory. Lacking the effects of speed

and surprise, the battle began to degenerate into that which Dempsey had wished at all costs to avoid – an infantry struggle.

By evening a Canadian division had cleared the southern suburbs of Caen, but by then the 11th Armoured had lost 126 tanks. The struggle continued for two days and finally a toehold was gained on the ridge. On 20 July, the rain poured down, the battlefield became a quagmire and Dempscy called off the attack. While on the map the results might seem hardly worth the losses, the British had finally cleared Caen and the Odon and Orne rivers were behind them. In spite of their own losses of over 5000 men and 400 tanks, they had so damaged the Germans that von Kluge had to admit he was losing the battle for Normandy. It was only a question of time.

The 20 July was a fateful day. The rains that soaked the 'Goodwood' battlefield caused Bradley to postpone 'Cobra', and in distant East Prussia, a bomb in a briefcase exploded in a failed attempt on Hitler's life.

The failure of 'Goodwood' nearly cost Montgomery his job: Tedder and other officers at SHAEF conspired to have him sacked.

One of the most successful weapons developed during the Second World war was the German 88 mm anti-tank gun. Originally designed for anti-aircraft purposes, its high-muzzle velocity gave it excellent penetrating power against armour plate. The photograph below shows the version designed to be towed, whose wheels were removed when firing. Other models of the gun were mounted on a self-propelled chassis, notably the powerful Königstiger tank destroyer.

Overleaf: map of the battle of Normandy showing the positions of the front line on 6 and 30 June and 1 and 15 August.

CHERBOURG

C O T E N T I N

Douve

VALOGNES   Quineville

Montebourg   Saint-Marcouf

Saint-Martin

Sainte-Mère-   Saint-Marie du Mont
Eglise

Barneville
Carteret

La Haye-du-Puits   Carentan   Isigny

Mont Castre

Lessay   Périers

Vire

Grandcamp   Pointe du Hoc   Vierville-sur-Mer
Saint-Laurent-sur-Me
Colleville
Port en B
Lo

BAYEUX

Balleroy   Tilly-su

Saint-Lô

Coutances   Condé-   Caumont
sur-Vire

Saint-Martin   *Odon*
des Besaces

Villebaudon

Le Beny-   Mor
Bocage

GRANVILLE   Villedieu les Poêles   Vire

AVRANCHES

Mont Saint-Michel   Pontaubault   Mortain

D

The front line during the battle of Normandy

❶ on 6 June
❷ on 30 June
❸ on 1 August
❹ on 15 August

LE HAVRE

Courseulles
Bernières
Douvres-la-Délivrande
Hermanville
Ouistreham
Merville
Cabourg

❶

Bénouville
Ranville
Carpiquet
CAEN
Troarn
❸
Hill 112
Cagny
Bourguébus
LISIEUX

Odon
Bretteville

Thury-Harcourt

❹
Falaise
Mont-Ormel

ndé-sur-Noireau
Chambois

Orne
ARGENTAN

ERS
❹

Sées

La Ferté-Macé

ALENCON

The air force commanders blamed him for promising decisive results and then failing to press the attack after their bombardment, while some American staff officers claimed that their men were taking the heaviest losses while the British sat around Caen doing nothing. This claim was patently untrue, but the controversy raged on in the background throughout the rest of the war in Europe. There was an added reason, however, for the urge for progress, as attacks on London and southern England had been started by German V1 pilotless flying bombs, fired from bases north of the Seine. Public opinion, and therefore the politicians, demanded an end to the menace, and it was easy for those in England to accuse the armies in Normandy of doing nothing.

The V1 – or flying – bombs (above) were launched by the Germans against London and southern England. Although many were intercepted by the RAF, enough reached their targets to cause political pressure to be applied for the launching sites to be dismantled as early as possible.

A jeep (below) from the US 2nd Armoured Division on a muddy track in the *bocage*.

'Operation Cobra'

While the British were embroiled in the carnage of 'Goodwood', the Americans had been engaged in establishing a solid start line. In this they were aided by a new device, called a Rhinoceros, developed by a clever young sergeant. To the front of a Sherman tank he welded several sharp steel

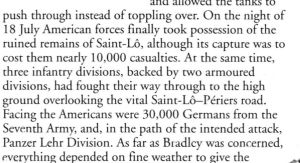

A Sherman tank (above) modified with a Rhinoceros cutting device.

prongs that bored through hedgerow walls and allowed the tanks to push through instead of toppling over. On the night of 18 July American forces finally took possession of the ruined remains of Saint-Lô, although its capture was to cost them nearly 10,000 casualties. At the same time, three infantry divisions, backed by two armoured divisions, had fought their way through to the high ground overlooking the vital Saint-Lô–Périers road. Facing the Americans were 30,000 Germans from the Seventh Army, and, in the path of the intended attack, Panzer Lehr Division. As far as Bradley was concerned, everything depended on fine weather to give the bombers a clear run to the target. The rain that had marked the final day of 'Goodwood' persisted, however, and Cobra had to be postponed to 24 July. Bradley is reported to have said: 'I'm going to have to court-martial the chaplain if we have much more weather like this.'

Nevertheless, the poor flying weather persisted and forced the attack to be postponed an additional day. Unfortunately, instructions were given too late to part of the bombing forces,

Disappointed by the failure of 'Goodwood', Winston Churchill (below) began to lose faith in the abilities of Montgomery.

RUPTURE DU FRONT
ET PERCÉE D'AVRANCHES 25 JUILLET 6 AOUT 1944

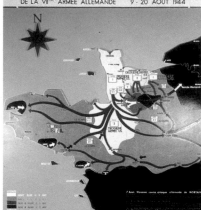

EXPLOITATION ET ENCERCLEMENT
DE LA VIIème ARMÉE ALLEMANDE 9 - 20 AOUT 1944

and several hundred tons of bombs were dropped, quite a few of them falling on the waiting troops, killing many, including a general. 'Operation Cobra' finally started on the morning of 25 July, but was again marred by bombing errors. One of the casualties was a lieutenant-general who had gone into the front line to observe; Bradley was furious at the ineptitude of the air force. Nevertheless, the bombing was a unpleasant experience for the Germans, and Panzer Lehr Division was severely damaged. Yet, as usual, the enemy put up a spirited resistance and on the first day the Americans advanced less than three kilometres.

The second day was equally indecisive. But, on 27 July, when Collins pushed an armoured division through the VII Corps front, the tanks drove into a vacuum and, much to their surprise, suddenly found themselves no longer facing any serious opposition. A decisive break-out had been achieved.

Waiting in the wings was the volatile General Patton, whose US Third Army his superior Bradley had scheduled to become operational on 1 August. Patton's presence in Normandy was a well-guarded secret, as he was still supposedly commanding the fictitious US 1st Army Group in Kent as part of 'Operation Fortitude'. Indeed, the German High Command still believed at this late stage that the 'real' invasion, which they thought

would be led by Patton, was yet to come. Patton was a cavalryman with a desperate desire to leave his mark on history. Bradley put him in temporary charge of VIII Corps and let him command the armoured pursuit that had unexpectedly been made possible. On 30 July the lead tanks drove southwards into Avranches, the opening needed for any move into Brittany, and then swung south to Pontaubault, where a bridge was captured intact. Disregarding his flanks, Patton ordered his VIII Corps to drive on into Brittany. An impressive seven divisions were pushed through Avranches in three days.

Les troupes allemandes contre-attaquent au sud d'Avranches

General George S. Patton, the legendary commander of the US Third Army, had been senior to Bradley in Tunis. In Sicily he had almost destroyed his career by slapping a soldier whom he accused of malingering in a field hospital. He was demoted. The battle of Normandy was for him a chance of proving himself.

Soldiers from the US 8th Infantry Division (left) march through the ruins of a village on their way to Avranches with the smile of victory on their faces at the end of July 1944. 'Operation Cobra' finally broke the lines of German resistance. While the German army concentrated its efforts against General Dempsey south of Caen, the tanks of the US 4th Armoured Division roared into Avranches and opened the roads to Brittany.

'Operation Bluecoat'

The British-Canadian front was not standing idly by during Bradley's attack. The Canadians had been ordered to attack Bourguébus ridge and, although repulsed, they maintained the impression in German minds that the real breakthrough would occur towards Falaise. Meanwhile, Dempsey moved the British VIII and XXX Corps westwards into the Caumont sector before mounting an attack – known as 'Operation Bluecoat' – towards Mont Pinçon and the Vire River. His aim was to cover Bradley's left flank, although his units would be operating in some of the most difficult countryside in Normandy. After heavy air bombardment the troops moved off on the morning of 30 July. They soon ran into stiff opposition, but by 1 August, the 11th Armoured Division was in possession of Le Bény Bocage and probing towards the town of Vire, which was unoccupied by the enemy at the time and could easily have been taken. Montgomery, however, assigned it to the Americans and the British withdrew. German attention was directed towards Avranches and they were thus caught off balance as their reinforcements had to turn to deal with the British penetration. The operation was marred by the fact that some of Dempsey's troops failed to push their attacks with vigour and the commanders of both XXX Corps and the 7th Armoured Division were dismissed.

Restructuring the Allied command and the counter-attack at Mortain

On 1 August there were a number of major changes at the top of the Allied command structure. Patton's US Third Army became officially operative on this date and Bradley was promoted to command what then became

the US 12th Army Group. Command of the US First Army was given to General Courtney Hodges. Montgomery's 21st Army Group now consisted of the British Second and Canadian First armies, the latter having become operational in July. He still in overall control of the campaign as ground forces commander – but from 1 August he was equal in status to Bradley. From this point on, however, the enormous preponderance of American manpower and equipment increasingly relegated British forces to a secondary role.

By the evening of 1 August the US 4th Armoured Division was in the suburbs of Rennes and the 6th Armoured was heading for Saint-Malo on the coast. So swift was their advance that it soon became obvious that much of the liberation of Brittany could be left to the French Resistance forces, leaving the US Third

A drawing (opposite below) of one of the rare night raids carried out by the Luftwaffe during the battle of Normandy. During 'Operation Bluecoat', the men of the 43rd Wessex Division finally succeeded in taking the high ground. Mont Pinçon was abandoned by the enemy on 6 August when von Kluge was ordered to withdraw his armour to prepare for a counter-attack towards Avranches All he could muster were the remains of four once-powerful armoured divisions. With British units firmly in control of the area south of the Orne River, there was a solid junction between the two Allied armies at Caumont.

General Courtney Hodges (opposite above), who took over the command of the US First Army from General Bradley on 1 August, was eclipsed by the volatile General Patton.

TYPHOONS & TIGERS IN THE FALAISE GAP

The Canadian army was given the task of capturing Falaise. Although the Canadians did not have to struggle through the *bocage* – their terrain was a flat plateau, ideal for tanks – they did have to contend with stiff opposition from the remaining Germans. In spite of massive preliminary air bombardment on the night of 7 August, progress was slower than expected.

Army free to turn east. Accordingly, Patton was ordered to head with the bulk of his forces towards Le Mans and then on to Orléans, south of Paris, as part of a general move to pin the German forces back on to the Seine.

Meanwhile, in the fantasy world inhabited by Hitler and his immediate entourage, plans were afoot for a massive counter-attack. On 2 August Hitler ordered von Kluge to detach all available armoured units, to assemble them into a strike force to be directed between Mortain and Avranches and to cut off the Americans in Brittany. In vain did von Kluge protest that his tanks were his only remaining defensive weapon. He was told to use eight of his nine divisions and was promised the support of one thousand fighter aircraft. His armoured units, however, were embroiled with the British and Canadians. By the evening of 6 August Patton's men were nearly into Le Mans and von Kluge had only disengaged four divisions. Moreover, it had become obvious to the Americans that something was afoot. Suddenly, during the night of 6 August, the Germans hit the 30th Infantry Division at Mortain without a preliminary barrage. Their attack was thus a complete surprise, but its thrust was blunted by American troops. The next morning the skies were clear and the Allied fighter-bombers easily sealed off the enemy penetration. Several more days of battle followed, but Bradley realized that he had been given a golden opportunity.

On the morning of 8 August, Bradley outlined a new plan to abandon the wide sweep towards the Seine,

replacing it by a manoeuvre that would trap the whole of the German forces between the Canadians moving towards Falaise, and Patton's XV Corps, redirected north towards Argentan. Montgomery enthusiastically concurred and a general mood of euphoria was evident among the Allied commanders.

The Falaise pocket

By attempting a counter-attack and – after it initially failed – refusing to withdraw, Hitler effectively signed the death warrant of the Seventh Army and the armoured units in Normandy. It was in fact in the Allies' interest to encourage the Germans to maintain their concentration in the Mortain area in order to give the Allies time to realign their forces for the planned entrapment. The British Second and US First armies were to maintain their pressure on the Germans in the centre, while, on the flanks, the Canadians were to push down the road towards Falaise. The US XV Corps would swing north from Le Mans to meet them and close the mouth of the pocket. Not a single German should have been allowed to escape. While the Germans moved their tanks west into the trap, Patton's armour headed east towards the Loire at full speed. To protect the flank of the counter-attack, von Kluge shortened his front

Subject to Hitler's orders, Field-Marshal Gunther von Kluge (below) was forced to watch the destruction of his remaining panzer units.

American troops (below) examine the blazing wreckage of a German Panther tank.

The Falaise pocket began to close and the area was turned into a vast killing ground as the fighter-bombers swooped down on the crowded roads. The surviving Germans were forced into the narrow valley of the Dives River, where the bridges at Saint-Lambert were still intact. Left: the wreckage of a German assault gun and other vehicles.

facing the British by withdrawing to a line running from Bourguébus, along the Orne to Thury-Harcourt and Mont Pinçon. While the Americans were capturing Vire on 6 August, Dempsey attacked Mont Pinçon in what was to develop into a bitterly contested small-scale battle. Once again losses in that difficult restricted terrain were heavy, but the high ground was captured, at the same time as was a viable crossing over the Orne at Thury-Harcourt.

The withdrawal of the German armour from the area near Bourguébus was the cue for the Canadians to mount an attack southwards on the night of 7 August. Although opposed only by infantry backed by a small reserve formed from the remnants of the 12th SS Panzer Division, the Canadian II Corps was still faced by the full weight of German heavy artillery and anti-tank guns. In order to avoid repeating past errors, the Canadian corps commander, General Simonds, decided to attack without a preliminary bombardment – and at night. His concentrated armour and infantry would thrust simultaneously across a narrow front, while aircraft would bomb the flanks to keep the defenders at bay. Shortly after midnight a thousand armoured vehicles set off southwards from Caen. When dawn broke they had penetrated nearly five kilometres through the first two

lines of defence, but then early-morning mist caused a delay. Several of the Canadian units and a Polish armoured division were inexperienced, and wasted time dealing with isolated enemy strongpoints, with the result that valuable momentum was lost. As it was, the Germans managed to reorganize, capably led by 'Panzer' Meyer in person.

That same morning Bradley directed his forces to attack northwards towards Argentan, as he was satisfied that he could control the situation around Mortain, where Hitler was still demanding that the momentum of the counter-attack be maintained. Von Kluge, unable to make any decisions without reference back to the Führer in East Prussia, realized the danger he was in but could do nothing about it – aware as he was of the price of disobedience. On 12 August the Americans took Alençon and by the following evening were close to Argentan, leaving a gap barely thirty kilometres wide.

The French General Philippe de Hautecloque (left), is better known under his *nom de guerre* Leclerc, which he adopted to protect his relatives in France. He was given command of the French 2nd Armoured Division that landed on Utah Beach on 30 July. The 2 DB, as it became known, was attached to Patton's XV Corps and took part in the final stages of the closure of the Falaise pocket.

French soldiers (below) of the 2 DB land in France on 8 August 1944 to help liberate their country.

LANDING IN S. FRANCE

"The Operation Is Going On Extremely Well"

Montgomery was putting pressure on the Canadians to storm towards Falaise and Argentan to close the pocket, but their path was blocked by the Germans' anti-tank guns. It was not until the evening of 16 August that Falaise was cleared of the enemy, and then the commanders on both sides began to worry about an accidental collision between their respective forces.

While the death knell was being sounded for the Germans in Normandy, the Allies were landing in the south of France

Initially the British, who felt that the manpower could be deployed more usefully in

Italy, were opposed to the operation. An American army corps, which included the French First Army, faced only light opposition and moved north up the Rhone Valley.

Meanwhile, in Normandy, the gap was still thirty kilometres wide and the Germans took advantage of it to withdraw, fighting all the way, to the Dives River. It was not until 19 August, when the Polish tanks and the US 90th Infantry met at Chambois, that the pocket was finally sealed off. In the process, however, the slaughter was terrible: 10,000 Germans were killed and 50,000 taken prisoner, while it is estimated that 20,000 managed to escape – mostly on foot and in small groups. Over the battlefield hung the stench of dead men, horses and cattle, and the lanes were choked with the wreckage of tanks, trucks and guns, the sad remnants of sixteen divisions. Barely more than a hundred armoured vehicles, harried all the way, succeeded in crossing the Seine. Patton was already over the river on 19 August, at Mantes, and three days later all four of the Allied armies had closed up along the line of the river. The Normandy campaign was officially over.

On 15 August Allied troops disembarked on the Côte d'Azure in the south of France. The operation had been the subject of much argument between the Allies as to its usefulness. In Normandy, a few days later, the Seine was crossed and the road to Paris was opened (above).

Many of the German prisoners were little more than children (left). In spite of their limited resources and the absence of air support, the Germans conducted a strong defensive campaign in Normandy.

DOCUMENTS

There are many actors in the drama of D-Day
– Allied leaders, soldiers on the ground,
sailors on the sea and paratroopers in the air;
French civilians and the French Resistance;
chaplains, war correspondents, medical staff –
people who made their own
individual contributions to the
greatest amphibious operation of all time.

A leader for 'Overlord'

In 1946, only a year after the end of the Second World War, the American General Omar N. Bradley started the task of writing his memoirs. As commander of the US First Army until 1 August 1944, when he became commander of the US 12th Army Group, Bradley played an important role in the Normandy landings. Here he gives his version of the structure of SHAEF and describes some of the personalities involved.

The selection of a supreme commander for OVERLORD had been under advisement as long ago as January, 1943, during the ANFA conference at Casablanca. At that time, when the cross-Channel invasion was being planned for 1943, it was anticipated that the assault would be primarily British. For that reason the conferees proposed that Britain name the supreme commander.

When the OVERLORD invasion was later postponed to 1944, British predominance in the assault gave way to the massive manpower reserves of the United States. Churchill stuck by his Casablanca declaration and recommended that now an American be named supreme commander. At Quebec the Prime Minister suggested to President Roosevelt that General Marshall be the man. If ever a man deserved the appointment, that man was General Marshall. Yet in the army hierarchy of command the appointment of General Marshall as supreme commander would have entailed a stepdown from his post as Army chief of staff. But stepdown or no, had General Marshall left Washington to go to Europe, no one – not even Eisenhower – could have taken his place....

In the end it was Roosevelt who made the decision to keep General Marshall at home....With General Marshall out of the running, the next logical choice for supreme commander fell upon the incumbent of a comparable post in the Mediterranean Theater. For after having defeated the Axis in Tunisia and Sicily, Eisenhower was now forcing his way up the Italian peninsula in that agonizing winter campaign. In terms of experience, tact

General Omar N. Bradley.

Roosevelt and Churchill, among others, at the Quebec conference in August 1943.

and perspective, Ike was admirably equipped for the job. Although some American subordinates thought him too ready a compromiser, especially in Anglo-American disputes, Eisenhower had demonstrated in the Mediterranean war that compromise is essential to amity in an Allied struggle....In early December Eisenhower learned from President Roosevelt that he had been chosen at Cairo to become supreme commander for the OVERLORD invasion. With only six months to go before D day, Ike wasted no time in forming the beginnings of a SHAEF staff from among his Mediterranean associates. If ever Eisenhower required an experienced and skillfully trained staff, it would be on the cross-Channel invasion.

To serve as deputy commander at SHAEF Eisenhower brought his first-ranking Mediterranean airman to England. A taciturn pipe-smoking Briton, Air-Chief Marshal Tedder had earned the trust and affection of his American colleagues in Africa by his modesty, skill and exemplary discretion as an Allied soldier....

As his chief of staff, Eisenhower named the brilliant, hard-working Bedell Smith, then with him in a similar spot at AFHQ in Caserta. Since England in 1942, the two had become inseparable partners. Although neither had grown excessively dependent upon the other, their relationship had been fused into so much an entity of command that it was difficult to tell where Ike left off and where Bedell Smith began....

E isenhower (above) and Montgomery (opposite).

To command the British 21st Army Group Eisenhower turned first to his good friend and Tunisian associate, General Alexander. Alexander had accompanied Eisenhower from Tunisia to Sicily to Italy where he commanded the Army Group comprising Clark's and Montgomery's Armies....

Had Alexander commanded the 21st Army Group in Europe, we could probably have avoided the petulance that later was to becloud our relationships with Montgomery. For in contrast to the rigid self-assurance of General Montgomery, Alexander brought to his command the reasonableness, patience and modesty of a great soldier. In each successive Mediterranean campaign he had won the adulation of his American subordinates....

Although I was unaware of it at the time, the British rejected Eisenhower's bid for Alexander and asked instead that he be retained in Italy to spark the peninsula campaign. Stumped on his request for Alexander, Eisenhower turned to Montgomery....

I had no premonition of difficulty with Montgomery in Europe. Though we often disagreed on plans and tactics, our working relationship was never impaired nor was our personal association unpleasant. While my judgment of Monty's achievements might be less rhapsodical than those of the British people, I shall never deprecate Montgomery's generalship nor his outstanding accomplishments in winning the war.

Monty's incomparable talent for the 'set' battle – the meticulously planned offensive – made him invaluable in the OVERLORD assault. For the Channel crossing was patterned to a rigid plan; nothing was left to chance or improvisation in command. Until we gained a beachhead we were to put our trust in The Plan....

Psychologically the choice of Montgomery as British commander for the OVERLORD assault came as a stimulant to us all. For the thin, bony, ascetic face that stared from an unmilitary turtle-neck sweater had, in little over a year, became a symbol of victory in the eyes of the Allied world. Nothing becomes a general more than success in battle, and Montgomery wore success with such chipper faith in the arms of Britain that he was cherished by a British people wearied of valorous setbacks....

Even Eisenhower with all his engaging ease could never stir American troops to the rapture with which Monty was welcomed by his. Among those men the legend of Montgomery had become an imperishable fact.

Omar N. Bradley
A Soldier's Story, 1951

Montgomery sets out his strategy for the Normandy campaign

My master plan for the land battle in Normandy...was so to stage and conduct operations that we drew the main enemy strength on to the front of the Second British Army on our eastern flank, in order that we might the more easily gain territory in the west and make the ultimate break-out on that flank – using the First American Army for the purpose. If events on the western flank were to proceed rapidly it meant that we must make quick territorial gains there.

On the eastern flank, in the Caen sector, the acquisition of ground was not so pressing: the need there was by hard fighting to make the enemy commit his reserves, so that the American forces would meet less opposition in their advances to gain the territory which was vital on the west....

Once on shore and firmly established, I began to get this strategy working and

after the heavy battles in the Caen area, and the overrunning of the Cherbourg peninsula, it began to take shape.

The Memoirs of Field-Marshal the Viscount Montgomery of Alamein, 1960

'Operation Fortitude'

The primary purpose of 'Operation Fortitude' was to conceal the real intentions of the Allies from the enemy by a variety of methods – by giving the Germans false information, by deceiving them about the date of the landings and, above all, by persuading them that the invasion would take place in the Pas-de-Calais.

The double agent Garbo

The plan, in broad outline, was to create two army groups, one real (21st Army Group) and one notional (1st United States Army Group or FUSAG). When the 21st Army Group went overseas, FUSAG would be left consisting of the US Third Army (real) and the British Fourth Army (notional). In the final stage, when the US Third Army had gone overseas, on about D+30, FUSAG would be left with only notional formations, these being eventually the Fourteenth US Army and the Fourth British Army. In the early stages before D-Day the map for the real order of battle showed the main weight of our forces in the Midlands, the west and the southwest; the false order of battle showed the main weight in Scotland, the east and the southeast.

The engineers built an illusionary army from rubber and wood. Below: a fake truck. Opposite: a dummy gun trailer and guard (top)and (right) a fake Sherman tank.

Once the false order of battle was firmly fixed in the German mind and the German files, the deduction on their part that the assault must come in the Pas-de-Calais area was inevitable, and there is abundant evidence that the Germans did in fact swallow the deception plan hook, line and sinker. A German map of the British order of battle as on 15 May 1944 which was later captured in Italy showed how completely our imaginary order of battle had been accepted and was largely based on the information supplied by the double-cross agents, especially GARBO and BRUTUS....

On D+3 GARBO, after a conference with all his agents, sent over a full report which he requested might be submitted

Rommel had pointed stakes ('Rommel's asparagus') planted in the fields of Normandy to hinder Allied gliders from landing there.

urgently to the German High Command. In this he set out in concentrated form the order of battle in this country, claimed that seventy-five divisions (instead of about fifty) existed at D-Day, pointed out that no FUSAG formation was taking part in the attack, and deduced that the real operation was only a diversionary attack shortly to be followed by an assault in the Pas-de-Calais area....

On 11 June (D+5) an appreciation was sent by Berlin to Madrid stating that 'all reports received in the last week from Arabel [GARBO] undertaking have been confirmed without exception and are to be described as especially valuable'.

It appears indeed that the Germans believed to the end of the chapter that the Pas-de-Calais attack was intended and would have been delivered if the Normandy attack had not been more successful than had been expected. Evidence of the movements of German troops entirely supports this view.

J. C. Masterman
The Double-Cross System, 1972

operations. Finally, added to all these were scores of smaller operations with exotic code names that would, it was hoped, distract the attention of the German forces from Normandy during the actual invasion....

On paper, 'Fortitude' was a magnificent fiction with which to surprise and confound the enemy. But would its stratagems work in practice? The enemy was clever, resourceful, powerful – and schooled in the dictum of the General Staff's greatest tutor, [military science scholar Carl von] Clausewitz, who wrote: 'A great part of the information obtained in war is contradictory, a still greater part is false, and by far the greatest part is somewhat doubtful.' Would the Germans remember that dictum, or could the Allied deception agencies convince them that the fictions of 'Fortitude' were both consistent with their own strategical and tactical beliefs and true beyond a shadow of a doubt?

Anthony Cave Brown
Bodyguard of Lies, 1975

LETTER FROM GENERAL EISENHOWER
TO WINSTON CHURCHILL
25 March 1944

The large-scale exercise which it is necessary to carry out 3rd–5th May will seriously detract from the degree of surprise that Plan 'Fortitude' is designed to achieve, if the enemy should interpret it in the true sense, as our final rehearsal. Accordingly everything possible must be done to convince the enemy that this exercise is the first, and that 'Operation Overlord' is the second, of a series of exercises which must be carried out before D-Day.

Dwight D. Eisenhower
Report by the Supreme Commander to the Combined Chiefs of Staff, 1946

Other parts of 'Fortitude'

There were other components to 'Fortitude'. The operation code-named 'Ironside' was designed to keep the German First Army occupied in the region of Bordeaux during the D-Day period by threats of an invasion along the Biscay coast; and 'Vendetta' was calculated to achieve the same result with the German Nineteenth Army in the region of Marseilles. The current phase of 'Zeppelin' would continue to put pressure on the Balkans during the D-Day period; and 'Diadem' was designed to pin down Hitler's army in Italy through orthodox military

Planning and training

From 1943 preparations for the Normandy landings began in earnest. Many thousands of American soldiers – many of whom had seen little active service – set foot on English soil to assist in 'Operation Overlord'. With their British counterparts they underwent a thorough programme of training to rehearse for the actual invasion.

An American soldier arrives in England

LETTER FROM CHARLES S. DEDON TO HIS PARENTS

25 May 1945

Our first glimpse of England was at the mouth of the Merci River, which we followed to Liverpool. It was dark when we landed and immediately boarded the train which took us to North Devon to a town called Mortehoe, it was near Woolacombe on the Bristol Channel. There we were assigned to the Assault Training Center. You may have heard about the place where the infantry received its training for the invasion.

The 453rd was the first Dukw [duplex-drive amphibious vehicle] company in the ETO [European Theater of Operation] and as a result was considered an oddity. Generals by the score came down to see us train and

A merican soldiers drinking beer at an English pub.

The truth about what really happened at Slapton Sands during 'Exercise Tiger' was kept a secret for many years.

operate and many of the later plans were based on the result of their observations. North Devon was an ideal place to be. The beach was large and resembled the French Coast to a certain extent. We were located in a Summer Camp which consisted of small cabins. They were like the tourists cabins found in the US.

We made many friends among the people there and spent most of our evenings in a small and old 'pub' called the Fox Hunters' Inn. It was run by a woman whose husband was a Wing Commander in the RAF. She was a grand person and many evenings after ten PM when the familiar 'time please' was sounded we adjourned to the parlor to finish our pint of bitters.

While there the company made a fine record for itself and assisted in training troops for the job ahead. We were on the beach from seven AM until after dark every day in all kinds of weather. We often felt the icy waters of the channel when a Dukw would go down or we would have to go in after somebody. It was an experience that was very valuable to our later operations in France.

Mémorial de Caen

The tragic exercise of Slapton Sands

LETTER FROM JOSEPH P. DOYON

4–7 June 1944

On 1 April 1944 we entered our first port upon arriving in England. The Harbor Master shouted over a loud bull horn 'Welcome Yanks to England'. He was on a large tugboat which was used to open the submarine net to let us enter the harbor.

We were given shore leave the next day and as I was walking down a street I felt a tug on my sleeve and saw a little boy about seven years old. He asked the standard question which all the children in England asked every American serviceman…'You got any gum chum?' You could not buy gum in England, and we always carried some. I asked the chap 'You got a sister mister?' He said he did, so I told him to go get his older sister and then I would give him a pack of gum.

Two hours later I felt a tug on my sleeve again and here stood the same little kid and he said I brought my sister. I looked at her and she was about nine years old. What I had hoped was his older sister would be at least a teenager....

Our next port of call was Plymouth, England where we had to unload a huge crane which had turned over onto its side due to the rough Atlantic crossing. It took special equipment and many hours. Because of this we were not able to go out into the English Channel for a practice landing with several other ships in our flotilla. It became a major disaster. Our ships went out without any war-ship escorts even when it was known that there were several German torpedo boats in the area. These boats known as 'E' boats were very fast and capable of speeds up to fifty MPH. Our top speed of the LST was fourteen MPH. About midnight the Germans located our ships and sank and damaged several others.

We were told of the incident in detail and threatened with a court-martial if we told any of the civilians when on shore leave. That night we lost 946 American soldiers and sailors. [Most sources give a figure of 700.]

History proves the best laid plans of men and mice sometimes go

afoul...It seems that our ships were on the wrong radio frequency when told the operation was cancelled, and not to proceed with the training exercise....

In the first week of June, all the naval ships were 'Sealed'. This meant no shore leave for any of us. The loading of troops and equipment had begun. From all over England, tanks, trucks, guns and troops converged on the south coastal ports. I think the whole southern coastline of England must [have] sunk down about two feet with all this weight.

My friend and I were sent ashore to pick up the mail and had stopped by the post office to talk with two friendly girls. They said that they did not believe that the Allies would ever invade Europe. The civilian populous

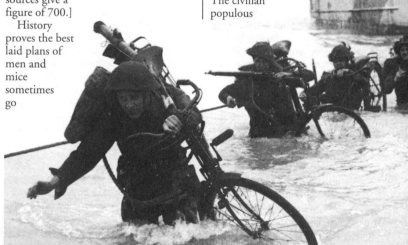

could certainly see the massive troop movements, so I often thought later that maybe the girls were pumping us for times and dates to be forwarded to German Intelligence. We did not tell them that our ships were loaded and we were invading the next day.

Mémorial de Caen

Training with bicycles

CORPORAL BILL BOWDIDGE, 2ND BATTALION, ROYAL WARWICKSHIRE REGIMENT

We were stationed at a camp in Sussex and we knew we were going to be among the assault troops on the invasion, but we didn't know where or when that would be. We knew that one of our roles would involve rapid movement because a few weeks before D-Day the whole company, from the commanding officer downwards, was issued with folding bicycles! I didn't think much about it at the time; when you're a junior soldier you just take whatever comes. I don't think anyone thought what are we doing this for?

I mean you're not paid to think, you just do it, accept it. I can't remember anyone saying 'What on earth are we going to use these for?'

There was time for us to take our bikes out on the Sussex roads to practise what we called 'cycle marches' – riding out in platoons like a pre-war cycle club, all bunched together, three abreast – and new drill movements were devised. The company would fall in in the usual way with the front wheels of our bicycles pointing to the right at an angle of fifteen degrees, the officers in front of their platoons holding their bicycles in the same way and the company commander, with his bicycle, facing the company. He would give the command to come to attention and turn to the right in column of route. To achieve this, we in the ranks would do a smart right turn and at the same time shuffle our bikes backwards and forwards so that they were facing in the right

British troops practise landing with bicycles during 'Exercise Fabius'.

direction. While this was going on the officers would wheel their bikes to take up position at the head of their platoons and the sergeants went to the rear. The OC would then shout over his shoulder, 'D Company, quick march!' and off we would go. After a few paces the order would be, 'D Company, prepare to mount,' and then, 'D Company, mount!' At this we would all swing our legs over and ride on, still trying to keep our dressing to the left. It was great fun.

Of course we had to carry normal marching order, weighing about fifty pounds, on our backs and consequently we all suffered from saddle sores.

Author's interview
Russell Miller
Nothing Less than Victory, 1993

Barbed-wire camps are set up to maintain secrecy about the invasion

LETTER FROM GUNNER ERNEST BREWER, G BATTERY, 5 RHA

28 May 1944

Dear Ma,

Well it looks as though I've well and truly had it now. We are all confined to this dump we have moved into; the camp is sealed – so they say. It seems a rotten trick not to tell us beforehand so that we could let you know that it might be our last time at home. I said it seems a rotten trick – rather it is. We are, so far as I can understand, kept here for security reasons, though I myself can't see what we could give away. We don't know anything.

Yours,

Ern

P.S. What's the betting on where we're going and when?

D-Day Museum, Portsmouth
Quoted in Russell Miller
Nothing Less than Victory, 1993

All southern England [in June 1944] was one vast military camp, crowded with soldiers awaiting final word to go, and piled high with supplies and equipment awaiting transport to the far shore of the Channel.... The southernmost camps where assault troops were assembled were all surrounded by barbed-wire entanglements to prevent any soldier leaving the camp after he had once been briefed as to his part in the attack. The whole mighty host was tense as a coiled spring, and indeed that is exactly what it was – a great human spring coiled for the moment when its energy should be released and it would vault the English Channel in the greatest amphibious assault ever attempted.

Dwight D. Eisenhower
Crusade in Europe, 1948

The Americans arrive in Britain

With them came luxuries such as chocolate and chewing gum. American affluence was also apparent in non-civilian life – in the quality and quantity of their uniforms and vehicles.

And then, suddenly, there were the Americans. There had been portents of their coming, in particular the appearance of a US Office of War Information booklet, snapped up by me from a town bookstall, on the Eighth US Army Air Force (USAAF), filled with photographs of the construction of the airfields from which it was to begin its bombing campaign over Europe, and containing a cut-away drawing of the Flying Fortress, for which, through counting the enormous number of machine-guns it mounted, I quickly formed almost as strong a regard as I already had for the Spitfire. There had been outriders, a scattering of officers in the unfamiliar rig of olive jacket and beige trousers – 'pinks and greens', as I subsequently learnt veterans nostalgically describe it – whom I used to see walking home on warm sunlit evenings to the lodgings which had been found for them on the outskirts of the town. On one of these, astounding myself by my forwardness and in flagrant violation of family rules, I tried the formula, which I knew to be in universal circulation, 'Got any gum, chum?' and was rewarded by an embarrassed halt – my embarrassment was altogether greater – a rummaging in pockets and the presentation of a packet of Spearmint. As it happened, I did not like chewing gum. But the superiority of the American over the British product, and particularly the sumptuousness of the wrapper and the lustrous simplicity of its design, instantly and deeply impressed me. Much of that evening, which would normally have been spent reading at a gap illicitly opened in my bedroom curtains, I devoted to a study of its elements, struggling in an increasingly trancelike state to draw from its symbolism the message which I sensed the designer sought to convey. Thus I made my first encounter with the science of semeiotics; but also with the bottomless riches of the American economy.

They were shortly to be made manifest in super-abundance. Towards the end of 1943 our backwater, which British soldiers had garrisoned so sparsely for four years, overflowed almost overnight with GIs. How different they looked from our own jumble-sale champions, beautifully clothed in smooth khaki, as fine in cut and quality as a British officer's – an American private, we confided to each other at school, was paid as much as a British captain, major, colonel – and armed with glistening, modern, automatic weapons, Thompson sub-machine-guns, Winchester carbines, Garand self-loading rifles. More striking still were the number, size and elegance of the vehicles in which they paraded about the countryside in stately convoy. The British army's transport was a sad collection of underpowered makeshifts, whose dun paint flaked from their tinpot bodywork. The Americans travelled in magnificent, gleaming, olive-green, pressed-steel, four-wheel-drive juggernauts, decked with what car salesmen would call optional extras of a sort never seen on their domestic equivalents – deep treaded spare tyres, winches, towing cables, fire-extinguishers.

There were towering GMC six-by-sixes, compact and powerful Dodge four-by-fours and, pilot fishing the rest or buzzing nimbly about the lanes on independent errands like the beach buggies of an era still thirty years ahead, tiny and entrancing jeeps, caparisoned with whiplash aerials and sketchy canvas hoods which drummed with the rhythm of a cowboy's saddlebags rising and falling to the canter of his horse across the prairies. Standing one day at the roadside, dismounted from my bicycle to let one such convoy by, I was assaulted from the back of each truck as it passed by a volley of small missiles, which fell into the ditch beside me.… But when I burrowed in the dead leaves to discover the cause I unearthed…a little treasure of Hershey bars, Chelsea candy and Jack Frost sugar-cubes, a week's, perhaps a month's ration, of sweet things casually disbursed in a few seconds. There was, I reflected as I crammed the spoil into my pockets, something going on in the west of England about which Hitler should be very worried indeed.

John Keegan
Six Armies in Normandy, 1982

The leaders

The guarded optimism of the Allied leaders – the British Prime Minister, Winston Churchill, and the American President, Franklin D. Roosevelt, on D-Day – contrasted with the disillusionment of the Germans – Field-Marshal Karl Gerd von Rundstedt and, later on, Field-Marshal Erwin Rommel.

The Allies

STATEMENT TO THE HOUSE OF COMMONS BY THE PRIME MINISTER, WINSTON CHURCHILL

I have to announce to the House that during the night and the early hours of this morning the first of the series of landings in force upon the European continent has taken place. In this case the liberating assault fell upon the coast of France. An immense armada of upward of 4000 ships, together with several thousand smaller craft, crossed the Channel. Massed airborne landings have been successfully effected behind the enemy lines, and landings on the beaches are proceeding at various points at the present time. The fire of the shore batteries has been largely quelled. The obstacles that were constructed in the sea have not proved so difficult as was apprehended. The Anglo-American Allies are sustained by about 11,000 first-line aircraft, which can be drawn upon as may be needed for the purposes of the battle. I cannot of course commit myself to any particular details. Reports are coming in in rapid succession. So far the commanders who are engaged report that everything is proceeding according to plan. And what a plan! This vast operation is undoubtedly the most complicated and difficult that has ever taken place. It involves tides, winds, waves, visibility, both from the air and the sea standpoint, and the combined employment of land, air and sea forces in the highest degree of intimacy and in contact with conditions which could not and cannot be fully foreseen.

Churchill and Montgomery conversing.

There are already hopes that actual tactical surprise has been attained, and we hope to furnish the enemy with a succession of surprises during the course of the fighting. The battle that has now begun will grow constantly in scale and in intensity for many weeks to come, and I shall not attempt to speculate upon its course.

This I may say, however. Complete unity prevails throughout the Allied armies. There is brotherhood in arms between us and our friends of the United States. There is complete confidence in the supreme commander, General Eisenhower, and his lieutenants and also in the commander of the expeditionary force, General Montgomery. The ardour and the spirit of the troops, as I saw myself, embarking in these last few days, was splendid to witness. Nothing that equipment, science, or forethought could do has been neglected, and the whole process of opening this great new front will be pursued with the utmost resolution both by the commanders and by the United States and British governments whom they serve.

Hansard, 6 June 1944

PRESS CONFERENCE HELD BY PRESIDENT ROOSEVELT IN WASHINGTON, D. C., ON 6 JUNE

President Roosevelt told a news conference, held thirteen hours after the initial announcement of the invasion of France, that the operation was proceeding according to schedule. He made this statement in a calm, rather low voice, but with obvious satisfaction that his composure did not entirely hide.

'How do you feel about the progress of the invasion?' a reporter asked.

'It's up to schedule,' Mr Roosevelt replied, then smiled.

This was the summation of all of today's dispatches as they were analyzed by the Constitutional Commander in Chief of the Armed Forces of the United States, who, since being awakened early with news that the invasion had started, had read reports and conferred with top-ranking officers.

Small losses are reported

The President added that, as of noon today, General Eisenhower had reported the loss of only two American destroyers and one LST (landing ship, tank), a heavy type of invasion barge. Losses of our air forces in the same period, Mr Roosevelt added, were about 1 percent of the airplanes involved. There was no figure on personnel casualties.

Other salient points emphasized by the press conference included the following:

1. Tentative dates for the invasion were set last December at the Teheran conference, slated in May or early this month, according to the weather.

2. General Eisenhower alone decided the actual date and place.

3. Marshal Joseph Stalin has known of the plan since Teheran and has been entirely satisfied with it.

4. A 'second front' a year ago would have been impossible because of lack of available men and equipment.

5. The war is not over by any means; this operation is not even over, and this is no time for over-confidence.

The President's press conference, a regularly scheduled one, was attended by 181 reporters, who filled the Executive Office almost to capacity. They found Mr Roosevelt looking tired around the eyes but smiling. He sat at his desk in shirtsleeves, wearing a dark bow tie. He smoked a cigarette stuck into a yellow amber holder.

Mr Roosevelt said that relatively few persons in the United States knew the tentative date for the invasion and that very few knew the actual date. He added that the actual date was set only a few days ago, being dependent on weather conditions.

It was largely a question of weather in the English Channel, the President emphasized. Longtime charts indicate that the first good weather each year occurs at this season, and for the invasion small-boat weather was necessary. He confirmed reports that the invasion was postponed for twenty-four hours at the last moment because of adverse weather.

When a reporter asked if the invasion of France was timed to occur after the fall of Rome, the President replied emphatically in the negative, saying that no one knew when Rome would fall.

The first consideration of this invasion, Mr Roosevelt went on, began early in 1941 in talks between himself and the chiefs of staff, and the plans have been consistently carried forward. Only military men, he emphasized, could understand the vast requirements for the undertaking, not the politicians who a year ago clamored for a second front.

He recalled that before the entry of the United States into the last war a political figure had said that America was always safe, because if this country should be attacked 1,000,000 men would spring to arms. The problem, Mr Roosevelt said, was providing the arms.

We had to wait and do what we could, he added, although the plans came gradually to a head, first at the Cairo conference, and afterward at

Teheran. The last six months of preparation particularly made a great deal of difference, with the vast additions of men and materiel to the forces overseas.

The President said that the choice of landing places had been made since the Teheran conference. He refused to be drawn into a discussion of possible other attack points or other matters of strictly military information.

Mr Roosevelt said he had no information as to how much surprise figured in the initial success of the landing operations; he also had no reports on operations by the French underground.

When he was asked to summarize his own personal reaction to the news, he said substantially that the whole country was extremely thrilled but that he hoped it would not develop over-confidence. He told reporters that you just don't land on a beach and walk to Berlin.

As for his hopes, he told a questioner he had only one desire, to win the war and win it 100 percent.

When a reporter told the President that an Axis radio station had broadcast yesterday that the invasion would not occur this month because Mr Roosevelt planned to go to England late in June the President shrugged and laughed.

The New York Times, 7 June 1944

GENERAL ÐWIGHT Ð. EISENHOWER

5 June 1944

Soldiers, Sailors and Airmen of the Allied Expeditionary Force!

You are about to embark upon the Great Crusade, toward which we have striven these many months. The eyes of the world are upon you. The hopes and prayers of liberty-loving people everywhere march with you. In company with our brave Allies and brothers-in-arms on other Fronts, you will bring about the destruction of the German war machine, the elimination of Nazi tyranny over the oppressed peoples of Europe, and security for ourselves in a free world.

Your task will not be an easy one. Your enemy is well trained, well equipped and battle-hardened. He will fight savagely. But this is the year 1944! Much has happened since the Nazi triumphs of 1940–41. The United Nations have inflicted upon the Germans great defeats, in open battle, man-to-man. Our air offensive has seriously reduced their strength in the air and their capacity to wage war on the ground. Our Home Fronts have given us an overwhelming superiority in weapons and munitions of war, and placed at our disposal great reserves of trained fighting men. The tide has turned! The free men of the world are marching together to Victory!

I have full confidence in your courage, devotion to duty and skill in battle. We will accept nothing less than full Victory!

Good Luck! And let us all beseech the blessing of Almighty God upon this great and noble undertaking.

The Germans

FIELD-MARSHAL KARL GERD VON RUNDSTEDT

The strength of the defences was absurdly overrated. The 'Atlantic Wall' was an illusion; conjured up by propaganda – to deceive the German people as well as the Allies. It used to make me angry to read the stories about its impregnable defences. It was a nonsense to describe it as a 'wall', Hitler himself never came to visit it, and see what it really was.

Quoted in Sir Basil Liddell Hart
The Other Side of the Hill, 1951

LETTERS FROM FIELD-MARSHAL ERWIN ROMMEL TO HIS WIFE

15 May 1944

Dearest Lu,

The middle of May already and still nothing doing, although a pincer attack seems to have started in Italy, which may well be the prelude for the great events of the spring or summer. I've been away for a couple of days, talking to the officers and men. It's quite amazing what has been achieved in the last few weeks. I'm convinced that the enemy will have a rough time of it when he attacks, and ultimately achieve no success.

10 June 1944

Dearest Lu,

…It is a hard fight that the army is having to withstand. I was up at the front yesterday and am going again today. The enemy's air superiority has a very grave effect on our movements. There's simply no answer to it. It's quite likely to start at other places soon. However, we do what we can.

14 June 1944

[Dearest Lu,]

Very heavy fighting. The enemy's great superiority in aircraft, naval artillery, men and materiel is beginning to tell. Whether the gravity of the situation is realized up above, and the proper conclusions drawn, seems to me doubtful. Supplies are getting tight everywhere. How are you both? Still no news has arrived.

The Rommel Papers
Edited by B. H. Liddell Hart
Translated by Paul Findlay, 1953

D-Day

The drama of those involved in the D-Day landings – the air, sea and land forces – on the five beaches comes alive here in accounts from British, Americans and Canadians, who were determined to prove themselves worthy of their mission. Their invasion threw the Germans off guard and showed up the deficiencies of the German chain of command.

Airborne operations – the Americans

I was 24 years old – a captain – in the 501st Parachute Infantry, a part of the 101st Airborne Division which, together with the 82nd Airborne Division, landed a total of 12,000 parachutists that night. We were the spearhead of the invasion of Europe. I realize that 12,000 sounds like a large force, but when you consider that we had been told there were 70,000 Germans there, you can see what the situation looked like to us....

For this performance our heads had been shaved – the surgeons insisted we'd be easier to sew up that way – our faces and hands blacked to be less visible. We wore a special jumper's combat uniform and boots. All of our clothing, including the long underwear and socks, had been impregnated with a chemical to protect us from poison gas.

We smelled like inside men from the skunk works. Our unique uniforms were made of a heavy cotton cloth – big pockets and lots of them with snap fasteners for quick opening – the jacket collars were high and right below the

neck we carried a switchblade knife in a pocket for emergencies like cutting yourself out of your parachute....

We also wore an equipment harness and ammunition belt with thirty rounds of .45 caliber pistol ammo and about one hundred rounds of .30 caliber rifle ammo, two hand grenades, a .45 caliber pistol, loaded and cocked, a .30 caliber folding stock rifle (carbine), loaded and cocked, a ten-inch blade knife strapped to the leg calf for hand-to-hand combat, a canteen with one quart of water, one spoon and canteen cup used as a cooking utensil, some water purification tablets, a combat first aid kit tied to the camouflage material that covered our steel helmets (special helmet liner required so helmet wouldn't be blown off in jump), special first aid kit containing two shots of morphine, sulphur drugs and compress bandages to stop bleeding. In a leg pocket we carried a British-made anti-tank mine because there were plenty of tanks nearby, a gas mask (I stuck two cans of Schlitz beer in mine), an equipment bag containing a raincoat, a blanket, toothbrush, toilet paper and six meals of emergency K rations – a combination shovel and pick for digging in; maps, flashlight, compass; also an 'escape kit' containing a very small compass, small hacksaw blade, a map of France printed on silk and $300 worth of well-used French currency. This kit was enclosed in a waterproof container measuring four inches by six inches by one-quarter inch- – everyone was encouraged to hide it in a different place on the body – I carried mine inside my sock, just above boot top on my right leg.

We carried two other items in our equipment. We wore our identification (dog tags) on a light metal chain around our necks, taped together so they didn't click or rattle. And at noontime before the invasion we had received our last surprise: A 'cricket'. This was a metal device made partially of brass and partially of steel. When you depressed the steel it made a snapping sound or a 'crick'. And when you released the steel part, it would crick again. This was...to be our primary means of identification between friend and foe during the night assault.... So with all this gear on me (the same for about 12,000 others), I was the third man to step out of plane #42, and dropping 800 feet to start what some have called 'The Longest Day'.

Sam M. Gibbons
Mémorial de Caen

Airborne operations – the British

For the airborne operations of the day the glider was essential. Only in gliders could guns, jeeps, scout cars, heavy ammunition and even tanks be transported. The glider needed no

American soldiers disembark from their aircraft behind Utah Beach on D-Day.

runway to land on, and was, on landing anyway, strictly expendable; most gliders crashed. They could stand up to very rough treatment but needed skilled handling....

The first task, the securing of the bridges over the Orne and the Caen Canal, was allocated to the [British] 5th Parachute Brigade, landing to the north of Ranville and clearing landing grounds for the Advanced Headquarters and anti-tank guns that would arrive later by glider. For the actual capture of the bridges they had under command a glider force of 180 men from the 2nd Oxfordshire and Buckinghamshire Light Infantry and from 249 Field Company Royal Engineers, commanded by Major John Howard. This force would take the bridges at midnight on 5/6th June by *coup-de-main.*

Major Howard's plan was to crash-land his glider force beside the bridges and overwhelm the defenders before the shock of their arrival wore off. This plan appeared to suffer a setback some days before the invasion when anti-invasion posts sprouted in the fields around the bridges, but his glider pilots were not a bit disconcerted. They considered they could use the posts to run the glider wings against and slow their landing speed....

Like most other airborne operations that night, Howard's task did not go entirely to plan. Of the 6 gliders, 4 landed on target, close to the canal and river bridges. One landed half a mile away. There were still enough men at Bénouville to do the job and James Wallwork describes the attack: '...The troops, encouraged by Major Howard, sang and (thank heaven) none was airsick. We were right on time and dead on target, thanks to our tug crew, and we saw the French coast in plenty of time to get set. Five, four, three, two,

one, Cheers! Cast off! Up with the nose to reduce speed while turning to Course I. That's when the singing stopped. We came in on the final leg at 90 miles [144 kilometres] per hour and touched down, crashing through several fences in the process and coming to a final stop half way up the river embankment....

'There was only one casualty on landing. The Bren gunner in No. 2 glider was thrown out and drowned in the pond in our field, about which everyone seemed to have avoided asking daft questions during briefing. Johnnie and I revived in a few minutes and with the aid of a medic I managed to crawl free of the debris.'...

Sergeant Roy Howard, heading for the Orne bridge, also had a successful crossing. 'We were at 1,200 ft and there below us the canal and river lay like silver, instantly recognizable. Orchards and woods lay as darker patches on a dark and foreign soil. "It's all right now, Fred, I can see where we are," I said. I thought that it all looked so exactly like the sand-table model that I had the strange feeling I had been there before....

'Up with the nose and then the heavy rumble of the main wheels as we touched down a few minutes after midnight close to the river bridge. "You are in the right place, sir," I shouted to Lieutenant Fox, who seemed both happy and surprised at the same time. With a drumming and crash of army boots, he and his men disappeared into the night.'

Robin Neillands
and Roderick de Normann,
D-Day, 1944: Voices from Normandy,
1993

The enemy reacts

About midnight, I heard the growing roar of aircraft, which passed over us. I

German soldiers in Normandy.

wondered whether the attack was destined once again for traffic routes inland or for Germany herself. The machines appeared to be flying very low – because of the weather? I looked out the window and was wide awake; flares were hanging in the sky. At the same moment, my adjutant was on the telephone, 'Major, paratroops are dropping. Gliders are landing in our section. I'm trying to make contact with No II Battalion. I'll come along to you at once.'

I gave orders without hesitation, 'All units are to be put on alert immediately and the division informed. No. II Battalion is to go into action wherever necessary. Prisoners are to be taken if possible and brought to me.'

I then went to the command post with my adjutant. The 5 Company of No II Battalion, which had gone out with blank cartridges, was not back yet from the night exercise – a dangerous situation. First reports indicated that British

paratroops had dropped over Troarn....

We telephoned the company commander, who was in a cellar. 'Brandenburg, hold on. The battalion is already attacking and is bound to reach you in a few moments.'

'Okay,' he replied, 'I have the first prisoner here, a British medical officer of the 6th Airborne Division.'

'Send him along as soon as the position is clear.'

In the meantime, my adjutant telephoned the division. General Feuchtinger and his general-staff officer had not come back yet. We gave the orderly officer, Lieutenant Messmer, a brief situation report and asked him to obtain clearance for us for a concentrated night attack the moment the divisional commander returned.

Hans von Luck
Panzer Commander: The Memoirs of Colonel Hans von Luck, 1989

GENERAL EDGAR FEUCHTINGER, COMMANDER OF THE 21ST PANZER DIVISION

I first knew that the invasion had begun with a report that parachutists had been dropped near Troarn a little after midnight on 6 June. Since I had been told that I was to make no move until I heard from Rommel's headquarters, I could do nothing immediately but warn my men to be ready. I waited impatiently all that night for some instructions. But not a single order from a higher formation was received by me. Realizing that my armoured division was closest to the scene of operations, I finally decided, at 6.30 in the morning, that I had to take some action. I ordered my tanks to attack the English 6th Airborne Division which had entrenched itself in a bridgehead over the Orne. To me this constituted the most immediate threat to the German position.

Hardly had I made this decision when, at seven o'clock, I received my first intimation that a higher command did still exist. I was told by Army Group B that I was now under command of Seventh Army. But I received no further orders as to my role. At nine o'clock I was informed that I would receive orders from 84th Infantry Corps and finally at ten o'clock I was given my first operational instructions. I was ordered to stop the move of my tanks against the Allied airborne troops and to turn west and aid the forces protecting Caen.

Once over the Orne River, I drove north towards the coast. By this time the enemy, consisting of three British and three Canadian Infantry Divisions, had made astonishing progress and had already occupied a strip of high ground about ten kilometres from the sea. From here the excellent anti-tank gunfire of the Allies knocked out eleven of my tanks before I had barely started.... I now expected that some reinforcements would be forthcoming to help me hold my position, but nothing came. Another Allied parachute landing on both sides of the Orne, together with a sharp attack by English tanks, forced me to give up my hold on the coast. I retired to take up a line just north of Caen. By the end of that first day my division had lost almost 25 per cent of its tanks.

Milton Shulman
Defeat in the West, 1986

Naval operations

Steady nerves were necessary as each ship edged up into her allotted position, finally checked by anxious navigators.

Still, everything was quiet ashore, amazingly enough; to a despondent mind it might seem more likely that the wary Nazis had some tremendous surprise up their sleeves rather than that they had been taken completely by surprise.... The extraordinary thing was that the Germans were caught off their guard. Among the first prisoners brought in, later in the day, was a German noncommissioned officer of a coastal-defense unit who was actually blown out of his bed by the opening shells of the bombardment – clear proof that the garrison was not on the alert....

Innumerable duels were fought out between batteries and battleships; it was kill or be killed – silence the batteries before the batteries sank the ships. In a few moments, there were great spouts of water leaping from the surface of the sea round the battleships to show how near the defending shells were falling. It was a supreme advantage for the ships to be able to move about; this disconcerted the German gun layers while it did not discommode the Allied gunnery control. A shore battery may be unsinkable, but it stays in one spot....

The extraordinarily efficient technical training of the Allied navies made itself apparent at once. One cruiser, the USS *Quincy,* scored five direct hits in successive salvos on a heavy coastal battery, silencing it....

With the bombardment at its height, three German destroyers came dashing out of the mouth of the Seine to see what was going on – another very definite proof that the Allies had achieved tactical surprise. They caught a single glimpse of the enormous fleet and fled immediately for shelter again....

Under intense fighter protection and in the absence of any serious attempt by the Luftwaffe to interfere with them, the spotting planes were able to execute their orders in a way an artillerist dreams about. It was thanks to them that the indirect fire of the battleships, rumbling over the cliffs of the shore and the gentle slope of the back country, was guided to its mark. Some of the observers' recorded comments tell their own story:

'Got him. Finis. Next target please.' And, after a 'straddle', 'That must be their headquarters. Generals running like billy-o.'…

But the solid, indisputable fact, evinced every moment of those anxious days, was that, at sea, America and England had an overwhelming artillery which could range deeper into the peninsula than any guns the Germans could bring up in a hurry, and that, furthermore, this artillery could be relied upon to hit its target accurately, hard and often. Military circles in Berlin, during the anxious days when the world awaited from hour to hour news regarding the progress of the invasion, commented bitterly about the 'red line' – the line drawn on the map marking the distance inland that the naval guns could reach. The vital part which naval bombardment played in the invasion

was a surprise to the world, just as it constituted a tactical surprise for the Nazis.

C. S. Forester
'History's Biggest Gamble'
The Saturday Evening Post
12 August 1944

Utah Beach

BRUCE BRADLEY, RADIO OPERATOR, B BATTERY, 29TH FIELD ARTILLERY BATTALION

I was attached to an infantry regiment that was to go in the first assault wave. We would be the first people to wade ashore on Utah beach…. We were told we were expendable in the first wave. I remember nobody responded to those chilling words. We were also cautioned to loosen our helmet straps as if we lost our grip on the rope ladders going down the side of the ship, we could plunge down with force enough to break our necks when the water hit the helmet rim. So I made sure I had a good grip. Better some battered knuckles than drowning. The sea was rough and it was dark. The navy guys had remarked that they were glad they were navy at this

S oldiers wade ashore at Omaha Beach.

point. I'm sure they were. We got V for Victory signs from them as they helped us over the side. Victory didn't seem possible at the time, to me. Survival, maybe.

Making the run into the shore the sky was intermittently lit by explosions, some of them of tremendous force. Bombs, shells from the battleships standing out to sea, rockets whooshing overhead, ack-ack from German positions and tracers were coming and going. An awesome display.

As we drew closer to the beach we could see the shape of the land. Also geysers of sea water were coming from shell fire, aimed at us. We had to keep our heads down. I remember I had been so tired from all the tension, lack of sleep, fear, etcetera, but all of a sudden I was not tired any more. I was very alert.

The noise of the shelling and counterfire was much louder, then there was a deafening blast and we were thrown down or knocked sideways. We had been hit by a shell. The coxswain was gone, the ramp was down, the boat was sinking. Sideways, I was thinking about how I would inflate my Mae West somehow. I did this automatically.

Most guys in that boat drowned.

My citation reads that I waded ashore, but the water was very deep and rough, so I dog-paddled toward the shore until my feet found sand. There were obstacles, triangular steel shapes, sticking up, but no barbed wire in my path. I waded onto the beach and hit the ground. I had lost my carbine, but still had the radio. I saw what looked like a low wall ahead and I crawled for it. Gaining some cover gave me a chance to pull myself together and assess my surroundings. To my right was a dead GI about ten feet away, to my left, about thirty to forty yards away, were some GIs in the process of regrouping. As I watched they went over the wall, so I decided to flip over it also. When I looked ahead, no more sand. It was a swamp of shallow water, but I was on my way, so I started sloshing forward....

Eisenhower Center
Quoted in Russell Miller
Nothing Less than Victory, 1993

Omaha Beach

So that all the ships would not arrive at the beach-head at the same time, we took a detour around the Channel

American soldiers being rescued in lifeboats off the coast of Normandy.

Islands of Guernsey and Jersey, and arrived at the Omaha beach around two o'clock that afternoon. The total number of ships involved was over 6950. This fact alone was unbelievable to the German coastal defenders. They had estimated a couple hundred ships at the most would have been available.

Our ship dropped anchor a short distance out from land because the beach-head area had not yet been cleared of mines, and roads had to be bull-dozed to get the equipment up off the beach....

On the way in to the beach, I saw one of our large ships sitting high and dry on the sand. It was an LST which was about 190 feet [57 metres] long. The bottom of it had been blown out by a mine. I felt very proud when I saw the American Flag, (Old Glory) blowing in the wind from the ship's mast. The Americans had landed, no doubt about it....

The beach was loaded with all sorts of equipment. Lots of oil, wrecked trucks, tanks, small boats, life jackets and bodies. Some whole, some not. I noticed a man's head that was no more than two inches [5 cm] thick. Another with his intestines strung out fifteen feet [4.5 metres] onto the sand.

Prior to the actual landings we were told that even though poison gas was outlawed, that if the Germans were ever going to use it, this would be the time. So when we sent in to the beach I was dressed in foul weather gear and had sprayed a poison gas repellant on all of it, including my boots. We also carried a gas mask.

We finally found a place on the beach that was clear of debris, and ran our boat up on the sand and lowered our ramp....

Joseph P. Doyon
Mémorial de Caen

For the D-Day landings Ernest Hemingway was assigned as a reporter to the infantry division of the US First Army.

Out a way, rolling in the sea, was a Landing Craft Infantry, and as we came alongside of her I saw a ragged shellhole through the steel plates forward of her pilothouse where an 88 mm German shell had punched through. Blood was dripping from the shiny edges of the hole into the sea with each roll of the LCI. Her rails and hull had been befouled by seasick men, and her dead were laid forward of her pilothouse. Our lieutenant had some conversation with another officer while we rose and fell in the surge alongside the black iron hull, and then we pulled away.

Andy went forward and talked to him, then came aft again, and we sat up on the stern and watched two destroyers coming along toward us from the eastern beaches, their guns pounding away at targets on the headlands and sloping fields behind the beaches.

'He says they don't want him to go in yet to wait,' Andy said. 'Let's get out of the way of this destroyer.'

'How long is he going to wait?'

'He says they have no business in there now. People that should have been ahead of them haven't gone in yet. They told him to wait.'

'Let's get in where we can keep track of it,' I said. 'Take the glasses and look at that beach, but don't tell them forward what you see.'

Andy looked. He handed the glasses back to me and shook his head.

'Let's cruise along it to the right and see how it is up at that end,' I said. 'I'm pretty sure we can get in there when he wants to get in. You're sure they told him he shouldn't go in?'

'That's what he says.'

'Talk to him again and get it straight.'

Andy came back. 'He says they shouldn't go in now. They're supposed to clear the mines away, so the tanks can go, and he says nothing is in there to go yet. He says they told him it is all fouled up and to stay out yet a while.'…

Slowly, laboriously, as though they were Atlas carrying the world on their shoulders, men were working up the valley on our right. They were not firing. They were just moving slowly up the valley like a tired pack train at the end of the day, going the other way from home. 'The infantry has pushed up to the top of the ridge at the end of that valley,' I shouted to the lieutenant.

'They don't want us yet,' he said. 'They told me clear they didn't want us yet.'

'Let me take the glasses – or Hemingway,' Andy said. Then he handed them back. 'In there, there's somebody signaling with a yellow flag, and there's a boat in there in trouble, it looks like. Coxswain, take her straight in.'

We moved in toward the beach at full speed, and Ed Banker looked around and said, 'Mr Anderson, the other boats are coming, too.'

'Get them back!' Andy said. 'Get them back!'

Banker turned around and waved the boats away. He had difficulty making them understand, but finally the wide waves they were throwing subsided and they dropped astern. 'Did you get them back?' Andy asked, without looking away from the beach where we could see a half-sunken LCV(P) foundered in the mined stakes.

'Yes, sir,' Ed Banker said.

An LCI was headed straight toward us, pulling away from the beach after having circled to go in. As it passed, a man shouted with a megaphone, 'there are wounded on that boat and she is sinking'.

'Can you get in to her? ' The only words we heard clearly from the megaphone as the wind snatched the voice away were 'machine-gun nest'.

'Did they say there was or there wasn't a machine-gun nest?' Andy said.

'I couldn't hear.'

'Run alongside of her again, coxswain,' he said. 'Run close alongside.'

'Did you say there was a machine-gun nest?' he shouted.

An officer leaned over with the megaphone. 'A machine-gun nest has been firing on them. They are sinking.'

'Take her straight in, coxswain,' Andy said.

It was difficult to make our way through the stakes that had been sunk as obstructions, because there were contact mines fastened to them, that looked like large double pie plates fastened face to face. They looked as though they had been spiked to the pilings and then assembled. They were the ugly, neutral gray-yellow color that almost everything is in war.

We did not know what other stakes with mines were under us, but the ones that we could see we fended off by hand and worked our way to the sinking boat.

Ernest Hemingway
'A Voyage to Victory'
Collier's, 22 July 1944

Determined to follow the Normandy landings, despite the objections to a woman war correspondent, Martha Gellhorn stowed away on a hospital ship that anchored off Omaha Beach.

June 1944

If anyone had come fresh to that ship in the night, someone unwounded, not

T he first casualties from Omaha Beach are taken on board a landing craft.

attached to the ship, he would have been appalled. It began to look entirely Black-Hole-of-Calcutta, because it was airless and ill lit. Piles of bloody clothing had been cut off and dumped out of the way in corners; coffee cups and cigarette stubs littered the decks; plasma bottles hung from cords, and all the fearful surgical apparatus for holding broken bones made shadows on the walls. There were wounded who groaned in their sleep or called out and there was the soft steady hum of conversation among the wounded who could not sleep. That is the way it would have looked to anyone seeing it fresh – a ship carrying a load of pain, with everyone waiting for daylight, everyone hoping for the anchor to be raised, everyone longing for England. It was that but it was something else too; it was a safe ship no matter what happened to it. We were together and we counted on each other. We knew that from the British captain to the pink-cheeked little London mess boy every one of the ship's company did his job tirelessly and well. The wounded knew that the doctors

and nurses and orderlies belonged to them utterly and would not fail them. And all of us knew that our own wounded were good men and that with their amazing help, their selflessness and self-control, we would get through all right.

Martha Gellhorn
'The First Hospital Ship'
The Face of War, 1986

Gold Beach

SIGNALLER I. G. HOLLEY, 1ST BATTALION, THE ROYAL HAMPSHIRE REGIMENT

I had already been in action in the Middle East and I felt like an old soldier, answering questions about what it is like. 'Brakey', one of our reinforcements was not yet nineteen and very apprehensive about going on his first operation. I tried to reassure him.

On our LCA there was a small keg of rum and a couple of bottles of whisky, put there by some unknown person, I never found out who, probably with the intention, good or bad, that we might need a little Dutch courage. One drink was enough for me, in the hope that it would settle a queasy stomach caused by the flat-bottomed boat tossing about in the swell. On board we had a naval sub lieutenant who, either from the magnitude of the event or from *esprit de corps* obtained from the rum, felt impelled to stand up and give forth a little speech on the great thing we assault troops were about to do.

Overhead there was the continuous whizz of naval shells homing in on their targets to soften them up for us. We were soon in range of mortars, a weapon we had grown to respect, and we could hear the sharp crackle of machine-gun fire. We had the word to get ready and tension was at its peak when the ramp went out. I was with the second in command of the company, a captain. He went out with me close behind. We were in the sea to the tops of our thighs, floundering ashore with other assault platoons to the left and right of us. Mortar bombs and shells were erupting in the sand and I could hear the burp-burp of Spandau light machine guns through the din. There were no shouts, only the occasional cry as men were hit and went down....

The beach was filled with half-bent running figures and we knew from experience that the safest place was to get as near to Jerry as we could. A near one blasted sand over me and my set went dead. (I discovered later that it was riddled with shrapnel). A sweet rancid small, never forgotten, was everywhere; it was the smell of burned explosives, torn flesh and ruptured earth.

High up on the beach a flail tank was knocked out. I saw B Company's HQ group take cover behind it as a shell scored a direct hit on them. They were gone in a blast of smoke out of which came cartwheeling through the air a torn shrieking body of a stretcher bearer with the red cross on his arm clearly discernible.

We got to the sea-wall, where Spandau from a pillbox to our left flattened us until it was silenced a few minutes later. We got on the road, running as fast as our equipment would allow. A Sherman tank had collapsed in a great hole, its commander sticking his head out of the turret going mad with rage. Past this we turned off the road through a wire fence with signs on it saying 'Achtung Minen'. A long white tape ran straight across the minefield, a corridor repeated twice again before we reached a cluster of trees where we were able to take stock of ourselves. There were six of us left.

D-Day Museum, Portsmouth
Quoted in Russell Miller
Nothing Less than Victory, 1993

Juno Beach

THE CANADIAN REVEREND MYLES HICKEY

Breathless, we stood and watched – and there before us broke the scarlet dawn!

Churchill tanks land on one of the British beaches.

No sun came up; the clouds hung low and dark; the waves rose cold and unfriendly like....

The beach was sprayed from all angles by the enemy machine guns, and now their mortars and heavy guns began hitting us. Crawling along the sand, I just reached a group of three badly wounded men when a shell landed among us, killing the others outright. That is why the report got around that I had been killed in action. Someone saw the shell hit and figured I had gotten it, too. The noise was deafening; you couldn't even hear our huge tanks that had already landed and were crunching their way through the sand; some men, unable to hear them, were run over and crushed to death. A blast shook the earth like an earthquake; it was the engineers blowing the wall.

All the while, enemy shells came screaming in, faster and faster; as we crawled along, we could hear the bullets and shrapnel cutting into the sand around us; when a shell came screaming over, you dug into the sand and held your breath, waited for the blast and the shower of stones and debris that followed; then, when it cleared a little, right next to you, perhaps someone you had been talking to half an hour before, lay dead.

Others, dying, might open their eyes as you reached them. By the little disc around their necks, I knew their religion. If Catholic, I gave them Extreme Unction with one unction on the forehead; but whether Catholic or Protestant, I would tell the man he was dying and to be sorry for his sins; and often I was rewarded by the dying man opening his eyes and nodding to me knowingly.

Reverend R. Myles Hickey
The Scarlet Dawn, 1980

Sword Beach

DR J. H. PATTERSON, ROYAL ARMY MEDICAL CORPS OF NO 4 COMMANDO

There was thick smoke over the beach, and the tide low but flooding. There were many bodies in the water; one was hanging round one of the tripod obstacles. The shoals were churned with bursting shells. I saw wounded men among the dead, pinned down by the weight of their equipment.

The first I came to was little Sapper Mullen, the artist. He was submerged to his chin and quite helpless. Somehow I got my scissors out and with my numb hands, which felt weak and useless, I began to cut away his rucksack and equipment. Hindmarch appeared beside me and got working on the other side. He was a bit rattled, but steadied when I spoke to him and told him what to do. As I was bending over I felt a smack across my bottom, as if someone had hit me with a big stick. It was a shell splinter, as appeared later, but it hit nothing important and I swore and went on. We dragged Mullen to the water's edge at last.

The Commando were up at the wire and clearly having trouble getting through. Hindmarch and I went back to the wounded in the water. I noticed how fast the tide was rising, and wounded men began to shout and scream as they saw they must soon drown. We worked desperately; I don't know how many we pulled clear, though it wasn't more than two or three.

'D-Day: A Second Opinion, A Medical Report of the Morning's Battle'
Lord Lovat
March Past, 1979

The battle of Normandy

After the euphoria of the initial landings came several weeks of difficult fighting for the Allied troops. Their advance was hindered by the bocage, *bad weather and strong resistance from German troops. However, little by little, the enemy crumbled. Finally, towards mid-August, victory seemed within grasp.*

A savage storm wreaks havoc on the artificial harbours

On the morning Collins jumped off for Cherbourg, we awakened to an ominous wind, a leaden sky, and a cold, scaly rain that tore at the tent flaps. Kean trudged with me to the mess tent halfway across the soggy orchard. He scowled at the weather from under his helmet. 'Well, this kills Collins' chances for fighter support today.'

Two miles beyond our CP, the Channel had broken into whitecaps and the surf foamed against the scarred cliffs of Pointe du Hoc. Storm warnings appeared in the weather report. But not until Wilson reported that unloading had closed down on Omaha Beach did we realize how serious was this crisis that had blown in with the storm.

On the eve of the second day of the gale, G-4 reported Omaha Beach strewn with wrecked craft as the Channel tumbled our shallow-draft vessels into junk piles on the shore. On the third day our artificial harbor on Omaha

A camouflaged German Panther tank waiting in ambush in the *bocage.*

Beach buckled under the pounding of the seas. The giant concrete caissons that had been constructed in England and towed across the Channel to provide an artificial harbor for all-weather unloading were now scattered across the Omaha Beach....

When on June 22 we went down to the beach to survey the damage, I was appalled by the desolation, for it vastly exceeded that of D-Day. Operations on Omaha had been brought to a standstill. Even the beach engineers had crawled into their damp burrows to escape the wind and the rain. In four days this Channel storm had threatened OVERLORD with greater danger than had all the enemy's guns in 14 days ashore. Hundreds of craft had piled up on the shingle where they lay mangled beyond the reach of the surf. Where we had landed on Easy Red [Omaha assault sector], a stricken rhino ferry stabbed into the side of another with each swell of the sea. The broken bow of an LCT lurched on a runnel as the seas boiled into its belly. Farther offshore another cowered helplessly as the surf foamed over the abandoned vehicles on its humped deck. A naval lieutenant in a Ranger's jacket ambled over to where we stood. I smiled wryly. 'Hard to believe a storm could do all this—' He looked carefully at my stars. 'General,' he said, 'we would much sooner have had the whole damned Luftwaffe come down on our heads'.

Omar N. Bradley
A Soldier's Story, 1951

An American surgeon remembers the casualties

In my memory today, those first few hectic, flaming days of battle seem a hopelessly confused nightmare. Nothing

American troops in the *bocage.*

seemed real, and days ran into nights and nights into days without meaning. Time almost stopped, and a week seemed like a month; but always in my mind I can see the never-ending stream of bleeding, dying, mangled boys whom the litter bearers brought in. In a matter of days all of us had become seasoned veterans of battle. Men rose to great heights and proved themselves men, or else went to pieces and revealed themselves as craven souls. Heroic deeds were commonplace, and usually went unnoticed.

Events seem hazy, and are not remembered clearly, but I do have painfully clear memories of watching so many of my friends come through the aid station. I hated to see the fine young infantry officers I had known so well and 'buddied' with coming in all shot up. I remember Captain Wheeler Coy (Battalion S-3), limping in with a nasty

American soldiers stand guard outside Cherbourg.

hole in his heel from a German bullet, frowning disgustedly at having been knocked out of the fight so soon, and looking so tired and worn. I remember Major Jastre (executive officer of the second battalion), gasping for air and turning greenish from a huge sucking chest wound, while I struggled unsuccessfully to save his life....

I remember the soldier who had watched with horror and terror as a lumbering tank rolled over his legs as he lay helplessly wounded on the ground. I remember the lad whose entire lower jaw was shot away. I remember the badly wounded boy who was brought in covered with mud and grass after he had lain unnoticed in a ditch for several days.

And I remember so many others, too. Casualties were far too numerous for us to evacuate by ourselves, and many of them were hauled back to us on infantry jeeps or were carried back by comrades on makeshift litters. One bit of mute

evidence of the tremendous number of wounded men treated in our station was the huge pile of discarded weapons outside. Before the injured boys came in, their weapons were dropped outside the station, and within a short time there was a large pile of Garand rifles, tommy guns, bayonets, trench knives, Browning automatic rifles, pistols, helmets, packs, blankets and so on....

To the uninitiated, it might seem strange that our division had so many casualties right away, but it is really not so surprising. We were all green, and inexperienced in war, so we did many things wrong. No matter how much soldiers maneuver and train, it takes the real thing to whip them into an efficient fighting force. Before long the 90th Division began to function like a well-oiled machine, but during those first few days all was confusion and error from top to bottom. It is always so in any division when it is first under fire.

Then, too, we were facing experienced German soldiers in well-dug-in defenses in this cursed hedgerow country, ideally laid out for defense. It would have been a tough job for combat veterans, but our untried troops were given the task. And so, many men made mistakes and were killed, but those who lived learned quickly by their experience.

William M. McConahey, MD
Battalion Surgeon, 1966

The commander of British 18 Platoon recounts the difficulties of fighting in the *bocage*

Normandy was a defender's paradise. It was bad tank country and our poor supporting armour lost many tanks, particularly to Panzerfausts (German bazooka detachments) firing at about thirty yards' [27 metres'] range or less. We soon learned not to allow our 'tame armour' to wander outside immediate infantry protection. In retrospect, Normandy is now a surrealistic dream, totally lacking the stark clarity of memories of subsequent battles: a pastiche of heat, dust, the stench of bloated cattle, the litter of dead tanks, rusting guns and wildly scattered grenades and small arms ammunition. We fought from one hedgerow to the next, up tortuous, overgrown sunken lanes: ideal country for the German defender but appalling for attacking infantry. However, no arm but infantry could take and hold the Normandy *bocage*.

It was here that I served my apprenticeship and the platoon developed its character which, despite constant depletion by casualties over the coming ten months, it would retain until the end of the war. It was also here that, imperceptibly, I became possessive with 18 Platoon. It was mine, to be guarded with an almost maternal jealousy that resented all criticism of my soldiers.

Most importantly, it was in the *bocage* that I began to appreciate how vital is grip: grip on oneself, grip on one's soldiers and grip on the situation. Unlike characters in novels and films, most men react nervously to real battle conditions. Discipline and regimental pride are supports but, indecisive moments of great danger, the grip of the leader on the led is paramount. Infantry section and platoon commanders must possess the minds and hearts of their soldiers. Strength of character is not enough. Successful leadership in battle, although complex and intangible always seemed to me to depend on two factors. Firstly, soldiers must have confidence in their leaders' professional ability and, secondly, they must trust them as men. It helps, too, if a leader has the reputation of being lucky. Field-Marshal Montgomery placed great importance on the principle of 'making the enemy dance to your tune'. Nowhere is this more important than in the platoon and company battle. It is decisive, because if you do not dominate events your enemy will....

Sydney Jary
18 Platoon, 1987

The German position

'Operation Goodwood' cost the British about 450 tanks. It was a masterpiece of preparation and logistics. And yet we were able to prevent the enemy from making a breakthrough.

Only now did we hear that on the day before 'Operation Goodwood' – the start of the offensive – our own Field-Marshal Erwin Rommel had been severely wounded in a fighter-bomber attack on his individual car. We could hardly take it in; to us Rommel had always seemed invulnerable.

Nevertheless, the deep defensive front set up by Rommel had held against Montgomery's attack. As late as 15 and 17 July he had checked this defense in the area of our corps. It is probably true to say that with this Rommel had denied his constant adversary the way to Paris, his last military success.

During the night of 19/20 July, torrents of rain set in, which made our relief more difficult. I shall never forget on our night march to the north the stink of the dead cows lying in the fields. On 20 July, moreover, there was a further heavy thunderstorm, which turned the battlefield into a swamp. The British air force had to stay on the ground.

Late in the evening of 20 July we learned – first through leaflets dropped by the British, then also from our own radio station – of the attempt on Hitler's life. The older ones among us had mixed feelings; the younger were angry, 'It's a stab in the back to us here at the front.'…

British soldiers west of Caen (above) and (below)

Although the RAF launched endless attacks and the guards division, with strong patrols, tried to find a gap to the east, the days that followed seemed to us almost like a holiday. Owing to the heavy downpours of rain the flooded River Dives had become even more impassable. For me the important thing was to recreate I Battalion, which had been almost wiped out by the bombing on 18 July.…

After only a week in our defensive 'resting' position the division was pulled out, to be restored to strength. We all hoped for a few days' peace to lick our wounds.…

Hans von Luck
Panzer Commander:
The Memoirs of Colonel Hans von Luck
1989

A British soldier describes how the liberators were received by the people of Normandy after 7 June

I entered Bayeux with the first troops. It was a scene of rejoicing as the people

at of German soldiers near Caen.

went wild. The streets were blocked with cheering men and women and children. The Tricolor and Union Jacks were hung in the windows. Cafés threw open their doors and pianists began to play British and French patriotic tunes. Crowds danced and shouted, 'Vive Tommy,' 'Vive l'Amerique'.

It was a scene of mingled war and peace through which I passed as I drove a jeep into the interior along part of the front line. After a dusty dreary morning, the sun burst through and the skies cleared. It was a perfect summer day. Driving through the coastal defense belt, I saw the havoc wrought by the Allied naval and air bombardment which had wrecked some roads and many hamlets which the Germans had used as headquarters....

In the fields peasants tended their sheep and cattle as if this day were no different from any other. The Allied war machine rolled past along the dusty highways, but the only sign the stolid peasants gave was a wave of the hand. It was the townspeople, like those of Bayeux, who really showed their appreciation, repeating again and again, 'C'est le jour de la libération.'

Richard McMillan
Quoted in W. W. Chaplin
The Fifty-Two Days, 1944

Montgomery believes his strategy was deliberately misunderstood at SHAEF

Many people thought that when Operation GOODWOOD was staged, it was the beginning of the plan to break out from the eastern flank towards Paris, and that, *because* I did not do so, the battle had been a failure. But let me make the point again at the risk of being wearisome. There was never *at any time* any intention of making the break-out from the bridgehead on the eastern flank. Misunderstandings about this simple and basic conception were responsible for much trouble between British and American personalities....

All through the fierce fighting which took place in Normandy, there was never any intention of breaking out on the eastern flank towards the Seine; reference to all the orders and instructions which I issued makes that abundantly clear. This false conception existed only at supreme headquarters and none of the senior officers responsible for the conduct of the actual fighting in Normandy, Bradley included, had any doubt about the true plan. The misconception led to much controversy and those at supreme headquarters who were not very fond of me took advantage of it to create trouble as the campaign developed....

Bernard L. Montgomery
The Memoirs of Field Marshal the Viscount Montgomery of Alamein, 1960

Recollections of the inhabitants of Normandy

The French people had a very different perspective on the Normandy landings. At first they lived through uncertainty and fear of the Allied bombings. Some towns, such as Caen, were razed to the ground. Nevertheless, the French citizens showed great courage and resilience in the face of hardship, and, finally, they were rewarded with liberation.

Caen: the town that was sacrificed

A tense atmosphere had reigned over this part of the country for some time. Rouen had been heavily bombed, as had many, many places on the Calvados and Channel coasts. Because of the constant gunfire, trains did not always reach their destination.

The Germans themselves were much more tense, changing the deployment of their troops and arresting a number of the Resistance. In this way many cells were disrupted and yet, on 1 June, the warning message for this area – 'the hour of battle is coming' – went out, followed on the evening of 5 June by the orders for action – 'the dice are down' and 'it's hot at Suez', Verlaine's too-famous line ringing no bells for the Resistance in Normandy.

A small group of maquis [member of the French underground movement in the Second World War who worked against the occupying Germans] to the south of Caen received its own messages. Even those people in Caen who had not been alerted, however, hardly slept that night of 5 June. From midnight on, enormous numbers of planes flew over the town. A little while before, the 1020th siren had sounded; though up to then Caen had not suffered from much bombing. This time, however, not only did the rumbling go on continuously but at about two in the morning the noise of heavy gunfire grew much worse and the sky was set ablaze towards the sea. At 0430 hours there was a strong impression that the Allies were clearing underwater defences and that the landing was destined for our beaches.

Citizens from Normandy taking refuge in Caen Cathedral.

Everyone pitied people living close to the beaches without suspecting that Caen itself would be in the front line for more than two months!

For some curious reason no one moved at the headquarters of the German 716th Infantry Division in the Rue Leverrier and the Avenue de Bagatelle. It was the only German division in the area, covering the coast from the Orne estuary almost up to Arromanches. It was said that its soldiers were not great fighters, though they had good artillery support; Russians made up two battalions and Caen only had a garrison of about 300 Germans who were very spread out. The first messenger to come and sound action stations only arrived at 03.30 hours and it wasn't until morning that General Richter and his men settled themselves in the bunker from which they issued orders against the landings.

Elsewhere in the guardhouse prisoners captured by the Germans were soon brought down from their cells in groups of six and shot in a small courtyard. Eighty-seven of them were counted. Only a few men were brought out alive the next morning.

Caen was already being bombed as the US 8th Airborne Division tried – with little success because of the cloudy conditions – to block the four main routes to the town.

The next morning there was a deceptive lull – the noise from the coast soon died down and nothing much happened apart from the infernal round trips of the Allied planes – the Germans hardly reacted at all. That day, in fact, not one German plane was to be seen; only the anti-aircraft defence went into action in a sporadic way. A strange atmosphere prevailed on the streets, with a kind

of bond being forged between those people who dared to go out. Very early on the inhabitants of Caen had taken the bakeries by storm and those who had taken the precaution of filling all their water bottles and cooking all they could congratulated themselves on doing so because the electricity went off and the water and gas were cut off very quickly and only restored six to eight months later!

Few Germans were visible, but we did not know that Allied aircraft had already spotted the movement of some armour from the 21st Panzer Division, which had been in the area for some time, and had also detected the start of the advance by Panzer Lehr in the Chartres region and by the 12th SS near Evreux. So when the Allied aircraft missed the bridges at about 13:30 hours, the fate of Caen was sealed.

The centre of the town had already been hit and fires had broken out. Then came that tragic night when tons of bombs rained down from almost a thousand bombers and the town was lit as if by daylight by flares hanging from parachutes. Many civil defence posts had been destroyed even before the rescuers could get there; many others were soon encircled by fire. In the Saint-Jean district, which was consumed by flames, rescuers performed miracles to save the wounded and survivors, particularly in the Misericord clinic.

By the second day all the firemen had been killed on active service or had been crushed to death in their fire station.

André Heintz
'Caen pendant la bataille: récit d'un témoin' in *Normandie 44*, 1987
Translated by Rosemary Stonehewer, 1994

A resident of Caen recalls the Allied invasion

Towards midnight I woke up, like everyone else, because of the dull sounds from the direction of the coast. Nobody was ever really surprised by this because we had suffered bombing raids nearly every day for several months. Meanwhile, the noise was growing hour by hour, the windows were rattling and you could see the Allied fighters by the jagged light in the sky. All along the ridge, which overlooked us, you could see blackish smoke clouds rising into the sky. The white heads of small balloons passed over the surrounding heights. The vibrations of the raid grew stronger and stronger. All over the neighbourhood, windows flew open, the shutters clattered and opinions were aired. There was no question of it: the landing had obviously occurred.

At 4 AM we all got up and bundled down to the cellar. Despite four years of waiting, nothing was ready – well, virtually nothing. Cupboards and chests were emptied in no time at all as bursting suitcases were piled up. The bathtub was filled with water as well as all available bottles. Activity was at its height.

The radio, listened to at 5.30, 6.30 and 7.30 AM, gave out not one detail. Only opinions flowed, the principal one being that 'a new phase of the airborne offensive' had just started. 'Please evacuate towns and villages within thirty-five kilometres of the coastline and as far as possible you will be warned of any raids.'

Eventually, at 8.30 AM, the announcer stated that 'the Grand Quartier general informs you that Allied troops have begun operations to land in the north of France'. Now the north of France for us

was Pas-de-Calais, so surely not our region. The streets of Caen were full of people, each with a bit of a smile, despite their anxiety. The noise was deafening, Electricity, water, gas, telephone – everything was cut off. Cars were driving at a most unfamiliar speed, no one showed up at work or few did. It seemed that life as we knew it was brusquely suspended....

It was about four in the afternoon and a few folks were gathered at our entrance gate, where there was lots of talk and discussions. Our neighbour, Madame Legrain, was determined to go out and look for bread, despite the reservations of her daughter, Antoinette. As for us, we decided to go around to another neighbour, Madame Vancoppenolle. We had hardly crossed her threshold when there was a horrendous drumming of heavy motors, Madame Gournay with her son and her mother dashed for the shelter under the stairs. The earth shook and through the window by the light of an explosion we saw the aeroplanes and their bombs falling to the ground, causing an appalling impact. Mother and I joined the others at the back of the room. Monsieur Gournay and Monsieur Vancoppenolle threw themselves to the floor. The whole company trembled as they prayed. Then came a second wave of bombers, more explosions and then silence.

Those of us who had relatives in town went to look for them in a state of great anxiety, seeking news of them. Mostly they found each other but Antoinette arrived at the house and threw herself into my arms. 'I've lost my mother,' she cried. 'I'll never see her again.' I did not come to that conclusion necessarily, but a little while later a covered handcart arrived with the body of poor Madame

Legrain. There were no more coffins
to be had, so M. Legrain made a coffin
from wood he found around his place.
The coffin was carried to the bottom of
the garden and put into the ditch dug
that very morning at the request of
Madame Legrain.

Madame Helene Hurel
Ouest-France, June 1984
Quoted in Russell Miller
Nothing Less than Victory, 1993

The Americans!

Thursday 3 August

When we were coming out of a café on
the square a strange car, filled with four
soldiers wearing khaki and large helmets
covered with green camouflage net,
arrived at full speed and parked under
the trees. They were Americans! One
of the men, a small brown-haired man
with a black moustache, stood up
and grabbed a telephone receiver, and
then talked while examining a map.
Everything seemed strange to me: this
nearly square vehicle, this telephone on
board a car, and, what is more, without
any wires!

A curious crowd quickly gathered.
We stayed silent for a second, as though
struck dumb, then suddenly we realized
at the same time what the presence of
these soldiers actually meant. Then
we all went mad. Cries of 'Long live
America!' 'Long live France!' 'Long live
de Gaulle!' rose, mixed, multiplied, soon
to be wiped out by the noise of the bells
which did not stop them. The bells
rang out with great clanging and there
was the enormous rumbling of an
interminable column of tanks. In
each tank a soldier, with a helmet on his
head and earphones on his ears, was
leaning out of the turret. He threw
out quantities of packets of sweets and

A part of Caen that was devastated by the
Allied bombings.

cigarettes. We did not join in the rush
unleashed by this hand-out, but all the
same we picked up a few packets.
M. Yver, laden with 'Camels' and
'Raleighs' was in heaven! He had been
rationed for many days, but now he
did not stop smoking.

Albert Desile
*Des sombres Années de l'occupation aux
chemins de l'été,* 1983
Translated by Rosemary Stonehewer,
1994

D-Day in film

The 1962 production of The Longest Day *was adapted from Cornelius Ryan's celebrated book chronicling 'the longest day of the century' (to use Rommel's words). Famous British, American and French film stars played roles ranging from the well-known battle commanders to the anonymous, but no less heroic, soldiers. In 1980 the courage of the US 1st Infantry Division, 'The Big Red One', was brought to the screen in a film of the same name directed by Samuel Fuller, who landed on Omaha Beach with this famous fighting team.*

Stills from *The Longest Day*: (top) a paratrooper near Sainte-Mère-Eglise; (above) Sean Connery in the role of a British soldier; (opposite top) paratroopers descend close to the church of Sainte-Mère-Eglise. Still from *The Big Red One* (opposite below): Lee Marvin as one of the American soldiers who landed on Omaha Beach. Overleaf: John Wayne (left) and Jeffrey Hunter (right) in stills from *The Longest Day*.

ALLIED CHAIN OF COMMAND

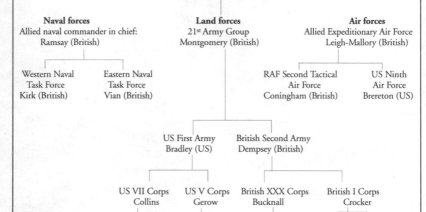

6 June 1944

JOINT CHIEFS OF STAFF

SHAEF
Supreme commander: Eisenhower (US)
Deputy supreme commander: Tedder (British)

Naval forces	**Land forces**	**Air forces**
Allied naval commander in chief:	21st Army Group	Allied Expeditionary Air Force
Ramsay (British)	Montgomery (British)	Leigh-Mallory (British)

Western Naval	Eastern Naval		RAF Second Tactical	US Ninth
Task Force	Task Force		Air Force	Air Force
Kirk (British)	Vian (British)		Coningham (British)	Brereton (US)

US First Army
Bradley (US)

British Second Army
Dempsey (British)

| US VII Corps | US V Corps | British XXX Corps | British I Corps |
| Collins | Gerow | Bucknall | Crocker |

Utah | **Omaha** | **Gold** | **Sword** | **Juno**

---

1 August 1944

SHAEF
Eisenhower

Ground forces commander:
Montgomery (until 1 September)

British 21st Army Group (British and Canadians)
Montgomery

US 12th Army Group
Bradley

| British Second Army | Canadian First Army | US First Army | US Third Army |
| Dempsey | Crerar | Hodges | Patton |

British VII Corps	Canadian II Corps	US V Corps	US XII Corps
British XII Corps	British I Corps	US VII Corps	US XV Corps
British XXX Corps		US VIII Corps	US XX Corps
		US XIX Corps	

GERMAN CHAIN OF COMMAND

6 June 1944

Hitler

Wehrmacht high command(OKW)
Keitel

Supreme commander in the west (OB West)
Von Rundstedt

Military governor of France
Stulpnagel

Naval Group West
Kranke

Air Fleet 3
Sperrle

Army Group B
Rommel

Army Group G
Blaskowitz

South of the Loire

Panzer Group West
Von Schweppenburg

1 SS Panzer Corps
Hausser

Fifteenth Army

Seventh Army
Dollmann

3rd Armoured Division
Reserve

partial control

1st SS Panzer Division
12th SS Panzer Division
17th SS Panzer Division
Panzer Lehr Division

XXV Corps   LXXIV Corps   LXXXIV Corps
Marcks

2nd Panzer Division
116th Panzer Division
21st Panzer Division

4th Infantry Division
+ 1 in reserve

ORDER OF BATTLE

THE ALLIES

Supreme Headquarters of the Allied Expeditionary Force (SHAEF)

Supreme commander: General Dwight D. Eisenhower (US)

Deputy supreme commander: Air-Chief Marshal Sir Arthur W. Tedder (GB)

Chief of staff: Lieutenant-General Walter Bedell Smith (US)

Allied Naval Expeditionary Force commander in chief: Admiral Sir Bertram Ramsay (GB)

British 21st Army Group

General Sir Bernard L. Montgomery (later Field-Marshal)

British Second Army
Commander in chief: Lieutenant-General Sir Miles C. Dempsey
I Corps: Lieutenant-General J. T. Crocker
VII Corps: Lieutenant-General Sir Richard O'Connor (after 1 July)
XII Corps: Lieutenant-General Neil M. Ritchie (after 30 June)
XXX Corps: Lieutenant-General B. C. Bucknall (after 3 August Brian G. Horrocks)

Canadian First Army
Commander in chief: General Henry D. G. Crerar (after 23 July)
II Corps (12 to 23 July): Lieutenant-General G. S. Simonds

US 12th Army Group

General Omar N. Bradley (after 1 August)

US First Army: Lieutenant-General Omar N. Bradley (after 1 August General Courtney H. Hodges)
XII Corps: Lieutenant-General Gilbert R. Cook
XV Corps: Lieutenant-General Wade H. Haislip
US Third Army: General George S. Patton Jnr
V Corps: Major-General Leonard T. Gerow
VII Corps: Major-General J. Lawton Collins
VIII Corps: Major-General Troy H. Middleton
XIX Corps: Major-General Walton H. Walker

Allied Expeditionary Air Force

Commander in chief: Air-Chief Marshal Sir Trafford Leigh-Mallory

Second Tactical Force of the RAF: Air-Marshal Sir Arthur Coningham
US Ninth Tactical Air Force: Lieutenant-General Lewis H. Brereton and Major-General Hoyt S. Vandenberg
Air Defence (GB): Air-Marshal Sir Roderick M. Hill
Commander of Bombers of the Royal Air Force: Air-Chief Marshal Sir Arthur T. Harris
US Eighth Air Force: General James H. Doolittle

THE GERMANS

Commander in chief: Adolf Hitler
Chief of staff: Marshal Wilhelm Keitel
Commander in chief and chief of staff: Colonel-General Alfred Jodl
Commanders of the west: Marshal Gerd von Rundstedt (until 2 July), then Marshal Gunther von Kluge (until 18 August), then Marshal Walther Model

Army Group B

Commander Erwin Rommel (until 17 July), Field-Marshal Gunther von Kluge (until 18 August), then Field-Marshal Walther Model
German Seventh Army: General Friedrich Dollman (until 28 June), then General Paul Hausser (until 20 August), then General Heinrich Eberbach (until 30 August)
Panzer Group West (until 5 August), later the 5th Panzer Army: General Geyr von Schweppenburg (until 6 July), then General Heinrich Eberbach (until 9 August), then General SS Joseph 'Sepp' Dietrich
I SS Panzer Corps: General SS Paul Hausser (until 28 July), then General Wilhem Bittrich
LXXXIV Corps: Lieutenant-General Erich Marcks (until 12 June), then Fahrmbacher (until 18 June), then Lieutenant General Dietrich von Choltitz (until 28 July), then Lieutenant General Otto Elfeldt

Luftwaffe (Air Force)
Commander: Marshal Hugo Sperrle

Kriegsmarine (Navy)
Commander: Admiral Theodor Kranke

THE DIVISIONS

The following divisions of each army were in Normandy on 6 June 1944 unless otherwise specified.

British 21st Army Group

British Second Army:
  6th Airborne Division
  Guards Armoured Division (28 June)
  7th Armoured Division (8 June)
  11th Armoured Division (13 June)
  79th Armoured Division (Specialized Armour)
  51st Highland Division
  50th Northumbrian Division
  Scottish 15th Division (14 June)
  59th Staffordshire Division (27 June)
  53rd Welsh Division (27 June)
  43rd Wessex Division (24 June)
  49th West Riding Division

Canadian First Army:
  4th Canadian Armoured Division (31 July)
  1st Polish Armoured Division (31 July)
  2nd Canadian Division (7 July)
  3rd Division

US 12th Army Group
US First and Third Armies:
  82nd Airborne Division
  101st Airborne Division
  2nd Armoured Division (2 July)
  3rd Armoured Division (9 July)
  4th Armoured Division (28 July)
  5th Armoured Division (2 August)
  6th Armoured Division (28 July)
  7th Armoured Division (14 August)
  2nd French Armoured Division (1 August)
  1st Infantry Division
  2nd Infantry Division (8 June)
  4th Infantry Division
  5th Infantry Division (16 July)
  8th Infantry Division (8 July)
  9th Infantry Division (14 June)
  28th Infantry Division (27 July)
  29th Infantry Division (7 June)
  30th Infantry Division (15 June)
  35th Infantry Division (11 July)
  79th Infantry Division (19 June)
  80th Infantry Division (8 August)
  83rd Infantry Division (28 June)
  90th Infantry Division (10 June)

German Army Groups B and Units of Army Group G
Seventh Army:
  77th Infantry Division
  91st Infantry Division
  243rd Infantry Division
  265th Infantry Division
  266th Infantry Division
  275th Infantry Division
  343rd Infantry Division
  352nd Infantry Division
  353rd Infantry Division
  709th Infantry Division
  716th Infantry Division
  2nd Parachute Division
  3rd Parachute Division
  5th Parachute Division

First Army:
  276th Infantry Division (29 June)
  708th Infantry Division (30 July)

Nineteenth Army:
  271st Infantry Division (24 July)
  272nd Infantry Division (24 July)
  277th Infantry Division (29 June)
  338th Infantry Division (mid August)

Fifteenth Army:
  48th Infantry Division (mid August)
  84th Infantry Division (30 July)
  85th Infantry Division (5 August)
  326th Infantry Division (30 July)
  331st Infantry Division (30 July)
  344th Infantry Division (mid August)
  346th Infantry Division (29 June)
  711th Infantry Division (29 June)
  17th Luftwaffe Field Division (mid August)

Foreign:
  Two infantry divisions (Norway and Denmark) and one Luftwaffe division (Netherlands) (after mid June)

Armoured Divisions:
  1st SS Panzer Division (late June)
  2nd Panzer Division
  2nd SS Panzer Division (late June)
  9th Panzer Division (early August)
  9th SS Panzer Division (25 June)
  10th SS Panzer Division (25 June)
  12th SS Panzer Division Hitler Jugend
  17th Panzergrenadier Division (12 June)
  21st Panzer Division
  116th Panzer Division (20 July)
  Panzer Lehr Division (8 June)

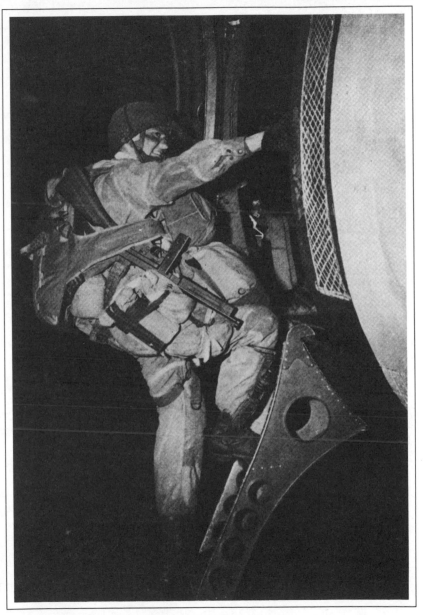

CHRONOLOGY

9 May 1939 Alliance concluded between Germany and Italy

1 September 1939 Germany invades Poland

3 September 1939 Britain and France declare war on Germany

1940 Churchill establishes Combined Operations to coordinate raids on the Continent and test methods of invasion

10 May 1940 German troops move into Belgium, Holland and Luxembourg

June 1940 Last British troops evacuated from Dunkirk, France

22 June 1940 France signs armistice with Germany and Italy

March 1941 First large raid carried out by British Commandos against Norwegian-owned Lofoten Islands

22 June 1941 Germany invades Russia

7 December 1941 Japan attacks American naval station at Pearl Harbor, Hawaii

11 December 1941 America enters the war

January 1942 Allied leaders confer in Washington, D. C.; large-scale invasion of France for early 1943 discussed

April 1942 Combined chiefs of staff meet in London to discuss a 1943 invasion of northwestern Europe during 'Operation Roundup'

19 August 1942 Canadian troops and British Commandos attempt a raid on the French port of Dieppe

November 1942 Allied forces land in North Africa during 'Operation Torch'

January 1943 Western Allies confer in Casablanca; chief of staff to supreme Allied commander (COSSAC) planning staff formed; invasion of France code-named 'Operation Overlord' postponed until 1944

31 January 1943 Gradual German retreat from Russia begins with the surrender of the German Sixth Army at Stalingrad

May 1943 At conference in Washington D.C., 1 May 1944 is set as new target date for Allied invasion of northwestern Europe (now code-named 'Operation Overlord')

10 July 1943 Allied forces land in Sicily

August 1943 American President Franklin D. Roosevelt and British Prime Minister Winston Churchill approve plans for 'Operation Overlord' in Quebec, Canada; Churchill proposes that an American should command 'Overlord', with the British taking supreme command in the Mediterranean

8 September 1943 Italy surrenders; Allies invade mainland Europe

December 1943 General Dwight D. Eisenhower is appointed supreme commander of the Allied expeditionary forces

January 1944 Southern counties of England turned into a vast military camp in anticipation of the Normandy landings

1 January 1944 Field-Marshal Erwin Rommel is appointed commander of German Army Group B

22 January 1944 American and British troops make an amphibious landing at Anzio, Italy

15 May 1944 Final review of 'Operation Overlord' by Allied chiefs at St Paul's School in London

4 June 1944 Powerful storm lashes the south coast of England and 'Operation Overlord' has to be postponed

6 June 1944 'Operation Overlord' is successfully launched on the beaches of Normandy

7 June 1944 British troops march into Bayeux

12 June 1944 American forces capture Carentan, a town at the base of the Cotentin Peninsula

13 June 1944 The British 7th Armoured Division fails to capture Villers-Bocage; first flying bombs land in southern Britain

14 June 1944 General Charles de Gaulle sets foot in liberated France

18 June 1944 American forces from the 9th Infantry Division take Barneville on the west coast of the Cotentin Peninsula; General Karl Gerd von Rundstedt and Rommel confer with Hitler at Soissons

19–22 June 1944 Severe storm wrecks prefabricated harbour, or 'Mulberry', serving American troops at Omaha Beach, and damages the British one at Arromanches

26–30 June 1944 British VIII Corps launches 'Operation Epsom' – the drive on Caen

26 June 1944 American troops capture port of Cherbourg

28 June 1944 General Dollmann, commander of the German Seventh Army, commits suicide

2 July 1944 Hitler replaces Karl Gerd von Rundstedt with Gunther von Kluge as supreme commander in the west

3 July 1944 Beginning of an American offensive to capture Saint-Lô

7–8 July 1944 British I Corps clears area to the north of Caen

17 July 1944 Rommel wounded and invalided home

18–20 July 1944 British forces secure area to the east of Caen during 'Operation Goodwood'

18 July 1944 American forces capture Saint-Lô

20 July 1944 Attempt to assassinate Hitler fails

23 July 1944 Canadian First Army becomes operational

25 July 1944 Beginning of Allied break-out from the beaches of Normandy during 'Operation Cobra'

31 July 1944 American troops capture Avranches; start of the move south into Brittany; British forces attack south of Caen during 'Operation Bluecoat'

1 August 1944 Allied command changes; General Omar N. Bradley becomes Montgomery's equal and takes over command of the US 12th Army Group; new US 3rd army formed under General George S. Patton; General Bernard Montgomery's 21st Army Group now consists of the British Second and the Canadian First armies

6–8 August 1944 Counter-attack by Germans at Mortain

8 August 1944 Canadian forces attack road between Caen and Falaise

12 August 1944 Argentan captured by US XV Corps under Patton

15 August 1944 Allied forces land in the south of France

16 August 1944 Canadian forces enter Falaise

18 August 1944 Field-Marshal von Kluge commits suicide; Walther von Model is named as his successor

19 August 1944 First units of US Third Army cross the Seine at Mantes

22 August 1944 Falaise pocket is eliminated by American and Canadian troops; over 100,000 Germany soldiers are taken prisoner

25 August 1944 Allied troops enter Paris

FURTHER READING

Ambrose, Stephen E., *Pegasus Bridge*, 1984

Bradley, Omar N., *A Soldier's Story*, 1951

Brooks, Stephen, and Eve Echstein, *Operation Overlord: The History of D-Day and the Overlord Embroidery*, 1989

Bryant, Arthur, *The Turn of the Tide 1939–1943*, 1986

Cave Brown, Anthony, *Bodyguard of Lies*, 1975

Chandler, David G., and James Lawton Collins Jnr, *The D-Day Encyclopaedia*, 1994

Crookenden, Napier, *Dropzone Normandy: The Story of the American and British Airborne Assault on D-Day 1944*, 1976

D-Day, Operation Overlord: From its Planning to the Liberation of Paris, 1993

D'Este, Carlo, *Decision in Normandy: The Unwritten Story of Montgomery and the Allied Campaign*, 1983

Eisenhower, Dwight D, *Crusade in Europe*, 1948

—, *Report by the Supreme Commander to the Combined Chiefs of Staff*, 1946

Funk, Arthur L., *Hidden Ally: The French Resistance, Special Operations and the Landings in Southern France, 1944*, 1992

Gellhorn, Martha, *The Face of War*, 1986

Hastings, Max, *Overlord: D-Day and the Battle for Normandy*, 1985

Hawkins, Desmond (ed.), *War Report: D-Day to VE-Day, Dispatches by the BBC's War Correspondents with the Allied Expeditionary Force 6 June 1944 to May 1945*, 1985

Hickey, R. Myles, *The Scarlet Dawn*, 1980

Howarth, David, *Dawn of D-Day*, 1984

Jary, Sydney, *18 Platoon*, 1987

Jefferson, Alan, *Assault on the Guns of Merville: D-Day and After*, 1987

Keegan, John, *Six Armies in Normandy: From D-Day to the Liberation of Paris*, 1983

Kemp, Anthony, *South Hampshire and the D-Day Landings*, 1984

—, *A City at War: Southampton in the Blitz*, 1989

Liddell Hart, Sir Basil, *The Other Side of the Hill*, 1951

— (ed.), *The Rommel Papers*, 1953

Lovat, Lord, *March Past*, 1978

Masterman, J. C., *The Double-Cross System in the War of 1939 to 1945*, 1979

McConahey, William M, *Battalion Surgeon*, 1966

Miller, Russell, *Nothing Less than Victory: An Oral History of D-Day*, 1993

Montgomery, Bernard L., *The Memoirs of Field-Marshal the Viscount Montgomery of Alamein*, 1960

Neillands, Robin, *By Sea and Land: The Story of the Royal Marine Commandos*, 1987

Neillands, Robin, and Roderick de Normann, *D-Day, 1944: Voices from Normandy*, 1993

Paine, Lauran, *D-Day*, 1983

Robertson, Terence, *Dieppe: the Shame and the Glory*, 1962

Ryan, Cornelius, *The Longest Day*, 1987

Seaton, Albert, *The Fall of Fortress Europe 1943-1945*, 1981

Shulman, Milton, *Defeat in the West*, 1986

Tute, Warren, John Costello and Terry Hughes, *D-Day*, 1974

Von Luck, Colonel Hans, *Panzer Commander: The Memoirs of Colonel Hans von Luck*, 1989

Wheldon, Sir Huw, *Red Berets into Normandy: 6th Airborne Division's Assault into Normandy, D-Day 1944*, 1982

Willmot, Chester, *The Struggle for Europe*, 1986

MUSEUMS

PRINCIPAL MUSEUMS IN FRANCE

Alençon

Arromanches
Invasion Museum, focusing on the landings and the remains of the Mulberry harbour

Avranches
World War II Museum

Bayeux
Battle of Normandy 1944 Memorial Museum, with a detailed exhibition of the battle, armour, uniforms, films and dioramas

Bénouville
Museum of the British Airborne Troops at Pegasus Bridge

Caen
Mémorial de Caen, a celebration of peace from the 1920s, including exhibitions, films, an exhibition on the Nobel Peace Prize, a library, archives, a cinema and lecture halls

Cherbourg
War and Liberation Museum, at Fort du Roule

Falaise
August 1944 Museum

L'Aigle
Museum of June 1944

Longues
Intact German coastal battery

Montormel
Memorial of Coudehard-Montormel on the battle of Normandy

Omaha Beach
American cemetery with more than 9000 graves

Ouistreham
Atlantic Wall Museum
No 4 Commando Museum on Sword Beach

Pointe du Hoc
Restored artillery battery, in memory of the US 2nd Ranger Battalion

Port-en-Bessin
Museum of the submarine wrecks from the landings

Quinéville
Liberty Museum

Sainte-Marie-du-Mont
Museum of the landings on Utah Beach

Sainte-Mère-Eglise
American Airborne Troops Museum

Utah Beach
Liberty Milestone, the first of a series of milestones marking the path of the US Army from Utah Beach to Bastogne

MILITARY CEMETERIES IN NORMANDY

American
Colleville-Saint-Laurent (9386 graves)
Saint-James (4410 graves)
British
Banneville-Sannerville (2175 graves)
Bayeux (4868 graves)
Brouay
Cambes-en-Plaine
Chouain
Douvres-la-Délivrande
Fontenay-le-Pesnel
Hermanville-sur-Mer
Hottot-Longraye
Ranville (more than 2000 graves)
Ryes
Saint-Manvieu (more than 2000 graves)
Secqueville-en-Bessin
Tilly-sur-Seulles (1224 graves)
Saint-Charles-de-Percy
Saint-Désir-de-Lisieux
Canadian
Bény-sur-Mer (2048 graves)
Bretteville-sur-Laize-Cintheaux (2959 graves)
French
Alençon
German
La Cambe (21,160 graves)
La Chapelle-en-Juger (11,169 graves)
Huisnes-sur-Mer
Orglandes
Saint-Désir-de-Lisieux (3735 graves)
Polish
Grainville-Langannerie (650 graves)

PRINCIPAL MUSEUMS IN BRITAIN

Bovington Camp
Tank Museum

Gosport
Royal Navy Submarine Museum

London
Imperial War Museum
National Army Museum
Royal Air Force Museum

Portsmouth
D-Day Museum
Royal Naval Museum

Southsea
Royal Marines Museum

PRINCIPAL MUSEUMS IN THE USA

Washington, D. C.
US Army Center of Military History
US Navy Museum

LIST OF ILLUSTRATIONS

The following abbreviations have been used: *a* above,
b below, *c* centre, *l* left, *r* right.

COVER

OPENING

CHAPTER 1

CHAPTER 2

CHAPTER 3

INDEX

Page numbers in *italics* relate to illustrations or references in captions.

A–B

ACKNOWLEDGMENTS

The author and publishers would like to thank the following for their cooperation in producing this book: Madame Chalufour at Tallandier; Madame Kuhl at the Bundes Archiv, Koblenz; the D-Day Museum, Portsmouth; the staff of the Imperial War Museum, London; the Figaro Magazine and Angelo di Marco.

PHOTO CREDITS

Archiv für Kunst und Geschichte, Berlin 13, 45a, 48–9b, 114, 125. BDIC, Paris 42–3. Bibliothèque Nationale, Paris 24c, 24–5, 43b, 63, 72–3b, 75, 94, 108, 126–7, 138–9, 150–1. Bildarchiv Preussischer Kulturbesitz, Berlin 14–5, 17a, 22, 76–7, 80b, 111, 177. British Film Institute, London 174, 175. Bundes Archiv, Koblenz 79, 80a, 89, 96a, 100b, 101, 162, 166b. Cahiers du cinéma 172a, 172c, 173a, 173b. D-Day Museum, Portsmouth 37a, 37b, 50–1, 72–3a, 82–7, 94–5, 122–3, 124. ECPA, Fort d'Ivry 44, 77. Imperial War Museum, London 15, 16b, 27b, 28a, 28b, 29a, 29b, 31b, 36, 38–9, 38b, 39b, 46b, 52b, 56, 57a, 57b, 70, 70–1, 76, 81a, 90a, 90b, 92–3, 103b, 104–5, 109, 119b, 131, 133, 136, 137a, 137b, 140, 142–3, 146, 167, 168, 183. Jean-Yves Brouard 21. Lapi-Viollet 17b, 30–1, 102b, 112, 122, 125. Magnum, Robert Capa 1–9, 11, 48–9a, 50, 54a, 60c, 78–9, 132, 155, 159, 164, 184. Mémorial de Caen 16c, 40–1, 47al, 47ar, 59, 61ca, 61cb, 62a, 62b, 65, 68a, 69, 78b, 95, 96–7, 98c, 104, 108–9, 119a, 120, 121c, 127a. Peter Newark's Pictures, Bath back cover, 14, 18a, 19b, 35, 39a, 58, 64a, 74a, 74b, 80–1, 88, 90–1, 97, 102a, 103a, 110, 120–1, 128a, 129b, 180. Roger-Viollet spine, 12, 22–3, 33, 41, 42a, 60–1a, 98a. Royal Air Force Museum, London 92. Royal Navy Submarine Museum, Gosport 32. Tallandier 18–9b, 20–1, 24al, 26, 27a, 30b, 34, 36–7, 43cr, 45b, 52–3, 54–5, 60–1b, 64–5b, 91a, 93b, 98–9, 100–1, 106–7, 107, 112–3, 118–9, 118b, 121a, 129a, 130, 134–5, 153, 156, 160, 163, 171, 175, 176. Tank Museum, Bovington Camp, Dorset 114–5. U.S. Army, National Archives, Washington D.C. 47b, 68b, 96b, 128b, 141.

TEXT CREDITS

Grateful acknowledgment is made for use of material from the following works: (pp. 168–9) François Bédarida, *Normandie 44*, 1987; reprinted by permission of Albin Michel, Paris. (pp. 132–5, 162–3) Omar N. Bradley, *A Soldier's Story*, reprinted by permission of the William Morris Agency, Inc., on behalf of the author © 1951 by Henry Holt and Company. (p. 139) Anthony Cave Brown, *Bodyguard of Lies*, © 1975 by Anthony Cave Brown; reprinted by permission of HarperCollins Publishers, Inc. (pp. 166–7) W. W. Chaplin, *The Fifty-Two Days*, 1944, copyright © 1944 by W. W. Chaplin; reprinted with the permission of Macmillan College Publishing Company. (pp. 146–7) Statement to the House of Commons by Winston Churchill, *Hansard*, 6 June 1944, parliamentary copyright. (pp. 140–1) Charles S. Dedon, letter of 1945 in the Mémorial de Caen collection; used by permission of the author. (p. 171) Albert Desile, *Des sombres Années de l'occupation aux chemins de l'été*, Editions OCEP/La Manche Libre, Coutances, France, 1983; used by permission of the publisher. (pp. 141–3, 156–7) Joseph P. Doyon, letter of 1945 in the Mémorial de Caen collection; used by permission of the author. (p. 144) Dwight D. Eisenhower, *Crusade in Europe*, 1948; published by Doubleday, a division of Bantam, Doubleday, Dell Publishing Group, Inc., New York. (p.158–9) Martha Gellhorn, 'The First Hospital Ship', *The Face of War*, Virago, 1986; reprinted by permission of Aitken, Stone & Wylie Ltd, London. (pp. 150–1) Sam M. Gibbons, manuscript in the Mémorial de Caen collection. (pp. 157–8) Ernest Hemingway, 'Voyage to Victory'; reprinted with permission of Charles Scribner's Sons, an imprint of Macmillan Publishing Company, from *By-Line: Ernest Hemingway*, edited by William White, copyright 1944, © 1967 by Mary Hemingway, originally appeared in *Collier's Magazine*, 22 July 1944. (pp. 160–1) R. Myles Hickey, *The Scarlet Dawn*, University of Toronto Press, Toronto, Canada, 1980. (p. 149) Sir Basil Liddell Hart, *The Other Side of the Hill*, Cassell, 1951; reprinted by permission of David Higham Associates Ltd, London. (p. 149) *The Rommel Papers*, ed. by Sir Basil Liddell Hart and trans. by Paul Findlay, 1953; reprinted by permission of HarperCollins Publishers Ltd, London. (p. 165) Sydney Jary, *18 Platoon*, 1987; reprinted by permission of Sydney Jary Ltd, Bristol. (pp. 144–5) John Keegan, *Six Armies in Normandy*, copyright © 1982 by John Keegan; used by permission of Viking Penguin, a division of Penguin Books USA, Inc. (pp. 152–3, 165–6) Hans von Luck, *Panzer Commander*, Praeger, New York, 1989. (pp. 136–8) J. C. Masterman, *The Double-Cross System in the War of 1939–1945*, Yale University Press; reprinted by permission of The Peters Fraser and Dunlop Group Ltd, London. (pp. 163–5) William M. McConahey, MD, *Battalion Surgeon*, Rochester, Minnesota, 1966; used by permission of the author. (pp. 143–4, 144, 155–6, 159–60, 170–1) Russell Miller, *Nothing Less than Victory*, Michael Joseph, 1993, © Russell Miller 1993; reproduced by permission of Michael Joseph Ltd, London. (pp. 135 and 167) Bernard L. Montgomery, *The Memoirs of Field-Marshal the Viscount Montgomery of Alamein*, 1960; reprinted by permission of HarperCollins Publishers Ltd, London. (pp. 151–2) Robin Neillands and Roderick de Normann, *D-Day, 1944: Voices from Normandy*, Weidenfeld & Nicolson, 1993; reprinted by permission of Weidenfeld & Nicolson Ltd, London. (p. 161) Dr J. H. Patterson, 'D-Day' in Lord Lovat, *March Past*, Weidenfeld & Nicolson, 1979; reprinted by permission of Lord Lovat. (pp. 147–8) Press conference held by President Roosevelt in Washington, D. C., on 6 June 1944, as reported in *The New York Times*, copyright © 1944 by The New York Times Company; reprinted by permission. (pp. 153–4) Milton Shulman, *Defeat in the West*, Martin Secker & Warburg, 1986; reprinted by permission of Reed Book Services Ltd, London.

Anthony Kemp
was born in 1939 and was educated
at Brighton College. He can clearly remember
the preparations before D-Day in the
Hampshire village where he lived as a child.
After service in the RAF, he spent several years in
Germany befo   grad   n modern history from
Pe broke College, Oxford
After a sh   a university ecturer,
he wo   as a researcher,
pr   and director of documentary
grammes f   British television.
e v asso i   ber o   d-winning
d ument   World War,
in   story of D-Day
       in-sur-Mer.
He i   books on   ous aspects
of r   and contemporary history, including
Sou lampshire and the D-Day Landings (1984)
and *A City at War: Southampton in the Blitz* (1989).

To Claude Quetel,
without whom it would not have been

© Gallimard 1994

This edition © Thames and Hudson Ltd, London,
1994

British Library Cataloguing-in-Publication Data

A catalogue record for this book is available from
the British Library

ISBN 0–500–30043–7

Printed and bound in Italy
by Editoriale Libraria, Trieste